Guide to
CENTRO ARCHIVES

Guide to
CENTRO ARCHIVES

40
CENTER FOR
PUERTO RICAN STUDIES
1973–2013

HUNTER CUNY The City University of New York

ISBN: 978-1-878483-83-6 (pbk.: alk. paper) - ISBN 978-1-878483-84-3 (ebook)

Published by

Center for Puerto Rican Studies
Hunter College, CUNY

695 Park Avenue, E-1429

New York, NY 10065

centrops@hunter.cuny.edu
http://centropr.hunter.cuny.edu

Art Design by: Reinaldo L. Ramos, Marcos Franco, José Alberto Quintana and Guillermo Vega

Printed in the United States

Guide to Centro Archives

The Center for Puerto Rican Studies (Centro) Archives:

The Jack Agüeros Script and Promotional
     Materials Collection
The Eddie Aguilar Photographic Collection
The Albors Photographic Collection
The Petra Allende Papers
The Bartolo Álvarez Papers
The Kathy Andrade Papers
The Rafael Anglada López Papers
The United Bronx Parents, Inc., Records
The Juanita Arocho Papers
The Genoveva de Arteaga Papers
The Arts Prints and Drawings Collection
The Carlos Arroyo Papers
The ASPIRA of New York, Inc., Records
Association of Hispanics Art AHA
The Asociación de Residentes y Descendientes
     Puertorriqueños en Cuba Collection
Ateneo Puertorriqueño de Nueva York (1962-1987)
     in The Diana Ramírez de Arellano Papers
The Juan Avilés Collection
The Alfredo Barela Collection
The Efrain Barradas Collection
The Rita Rivera Barreto Collection
Records of El Barrio Popular Education Program
The Pura Belpré Papers
The Records of El Bohio Community and Cultural Center, Inc.
The Frank Bonilla Papers
The Records of the Bureau of Identification, 1930-1948
The Joseph A. Burgos Collection
The Jose Buscaglia Collection
The Buttons Collection
The Diana Caballero Papers
The Susanne Cabañas Collection
The Gonzalo Cabassa Ramírez Collection
The Elba Cabrera Papers
California Puerto Rican Historical Society West Coast
     Oral History Project Collection
The Blase Camacho Souza Papers
The Taína Caragol Art Catalogs Collection
The Alice Cardona Papers
The Luis A. Cardona Oral History Collection
Caribbean Cultural Center Photographs
The John Carro Collection
The Rudy Castilla Photographs Collection
Centro de Estudios Puertorriqueños Records (CENTRO)
Josefina Cintrón Collection
The Records of CHARAS

The Claridad Bilingüe Collection, 1971-1985
The Club Puertorriqueño de San Francisco Minutes
The Clara Colón Papers
The Jesus Colón Papers
The Joaquín Colón Lopez Papers
The Máximo Colón Photographic Collection
The Miriam Colón Collection
The Ramón Colón Papers
The Yarisa Colón Art Books Collection
The Gilberto Concepción de Gracia New York Years Collection
The Helen Conde Pérez Collection
The Joe Conzo Collection
The Félix L. Cordero Meléndez Collection
The Félix Cordero Collection
The María Cortijo Collection
The Marithelma Costa Interviews Collection
Cuatro Center Project Collection
The Pura Cruz Collection
CUNY Association of Caribbean Studies Collection, 1985-1986
The Edgar de Jesús Papers
The Ramón Delgado Papers
The Efraín Díaz Santiago Iglesias Educational Society Collection
The Manuel Díaz Papers
The William Díaz Papers
The Records of the Department of the Puerto Rican Community
     Affairs, 1989-1993
The Doval Family Collection

East Harlem Common Ground Collection
East Harlem Council for Community Improvement Inc., Records
The Diego Echevarría Audiovisual Collection
The Sandra Esteves Collection
The Aníbal Félix Papers
The Fernando Ferrer Electoral Campaign Collection
The Víctor Fragoso Collection
The Fragoza Family Collection
The Oscar García Rivera Papers
The Robert Garcia Congressional Papers
The Samuel García Papers
The Sandra García-Rivera Papers
The Gilberto Gerena Valentín Papers
The Ruth Glasser Musicians Interview Collection
The Enrique Gómez Collection
The Carmen González Papers
The Edward González Papers
The Juan Gonzalez Papers

Foreword

I t is my great pleasure to introduce this special Centro Archives publication. The collections reflect the diversity, talent and richness of the Puerto Rican communities in the U.S. It also documents the generosity of so many who entrusted their papers and organizational records to our institution. To all of them we extend our most sincere gratitude.

Thanks to the City University of New York and Hunter College for their ongoing support of the Centro Archives, the only archival repository in the United States exclusively devoted to documenting the Puerto Rican communities living in this country. The Archives' contribution to the academic fields of Puerto Rican, Latino and American studies has been significant.

I am especially grateful to our Archives team for their dedication to preserving Puerto Rican history on a daily basis. Special thanks to Pedro Juan Hernández, Diego Valencia, Ana Rosa Pérez, Jonathan Morales and Madonna Hernández. This project was designed by Reinaldo Ramos, Guillermo Vega, José Alberto Quintana and Marcos Franco, students from the School of Architecture of the Catholic University of Puerto Rico, Ponce currently participating in a pilot exchange program at Centro.

Our task is not an easy one. In order to share and preserve their histories for future generations of researchers, scholars, students and the public in general who may want to discover the treasures hidden within these collections, we need to identify, organize, process and preserve thousands of materials such as books, letters, journals, newspapers, theses, music and audio visual materials and make them accessible to all.

We invite you to come and visit our facilities. Discover new fascinating stories of people who, like many of us, faced the challenges of relocation and daily life in communities like New York, Chicago, Boston and Orlando. The opportunities in such places, along with their extraordinary diversity, made it possible to call them home.

Dr. Alberto Hernández-Banuchi
Centro Associate Director
Chief Librarian & Archivist

Introduction

The Center for Puerto Rican Studies is a research institute based at Hunter College, of the City University of New York, with the mission of conducting and supporting research on the Puerto Rican experience in the United States. The Centro Archives is the only archival repository nationwide exclusively devoted to documenting the Puerto Rican communities living in the United States. Its holdings include books, newspapers and journals, miscellaneous ephemeral materials, personal and government papers, graphics, special collections, documents and oral histories. It provides reference and research materials to students and faculty throughout CUNY and other academic institutions, as well as to independent researchers and the general community.

The Centro Archives program was formally established in 1989 when it reached professional archival standards. Since then, it has created a unique national collection exclusively devoted to the dissemination of information from varied perspectives on Puerto Ricans in the United States. Since its inception, Centro Archives staff have been dedicated to gathering and identifying many types of documents, and arranging and describing their content in order to share and preserve these important resources. The Centro Archives' value is recognized by those individuals and organizations who continue to graciously donate their papers and records, as well as external professional bodies, such as the Boards of Regents, the New York State Department of Education, and the New York State Archives and Records Administration, who awarded the Centro Archives their awards for excellence in historical records repository and in documenting New York's history in 1994 and 2002. The Centro Archives have grown from less than 200 cubic feet at the beginning to over 6,000 cubic feet today. Centro Archives has become a nationwide hub where a diverse community of scholars and researchers meet to document and share their findings.

The close to 300 collections in Centro Archives include the personal papers and records of organizations with dates spanning from the 1910s to the present. The primary focuses of the collections are in the areas of social history, culture and the arts. While most of the archival collections document the lives of Puerto Ricans in New York City, there are also collections documenting the migrations to Florida, California, Hawaii, and other Northeast and Midwest locations. Among our holdings there are close to 100,000 photographs and negatives, 2,000 art and political posters, drawings and other materials, 2,000 videos, 2,000 audio recordings, 1,300 Long Play vinyl records, 1,000 postcards, 316 buttons from political and cultural events, over 100 maps, and 20 16 mm short films.

The largest Centro Archives record collections are from the Offices of the Government of Puerto Rico in the United States (OGPRUS), an unparalleled resource on the history of Puerto Rican migration containing an extraordinary amount of information about individual migrants and the institutions set up by the government to assist them. These records document the functions of the Bureau of Identification and Documentation, 1930-1948; the Office of Information for Puerto Rico, 1945-1949; the Migration Division from 1948 to 1989; and also the Department of Community Affairs in the United States, 1989-1993, a cabinet-level department, which superseded the Migration Division.

Other large record collections are those of the Puerto Rican Legal Defense and Education Fund (now Latino Justice), ASPIRA of New York, and the United Bronx Parents, Inc. Organizations that continue to play an essential role within the Puerto Rican community. Centro's own organizational records, in conjunction with the papers of its first director Frank Bonilla, are also an important resource about the intellectual production of a research center, its creativity, struggle, politics and leadership that created a vital academic and community resource.

The first major individual collection acquired by the Archives, the Jesús Colón Papers (1901-1974), makes a significant contribution to the study of Puerto Rican history and is essential to the reconstruction of the history of the Puerto Rican community in New York in the 20th century. Colón was a tireless community leader and writer whose papers support research on organizational development and political participation in New York City. The papers shed light on issues of employment, discrimination and relationships of Puerto Ricans with other groups, as well as the history of the labor movement on the island and its political nvolvement in New York.

The Archives are the repository of the papers of two recipients of the highest civilian awards in the country: Dr. Antonia Pantoja, Presidential Medal of Freedom (1996); and Dr. Helen Rodríguez Trías, Presidential Citizens Medal (2001). Pantoja, an iconic figure in the Puerto Rican community, reigns as one of the leaders in community development and as a key figure in the founding of several seminal Puerto Rican institutions. Rodríguez Trías was a noted pediatrician, public health leader and women's rights activist who worked tirelessly throughout her career to expand the range of health care services available to women and children, especially those in underserved and marginalized communities in Puerto Rico and across the United States.

Among our most sought-after collections by researchers are those of New York State Assemblyman Oscar García Rivera, the first Puerto Rican elected to public office in the continental United States, former U.S. Congressman Robert Garcia, as well as those of writers Clemente Soto Vélez, Pedro Pietri, Edgardo Vega Yunqué, and Pura Belpré. The Justo Martí Collection, a photograph collection which captures various aspects of family life, communities, and the activities of social and political Puerto Rican and Latino organizations, is especially prized by reseachers.

Many of the collections in our archives demand different research approaches and summon us to explore new strategies and dimensions in order to have a better understanding of our resilient community. They also invite us to build relationships with living communities and other archival repositories throughout the United States.

As an example, a second generation Puerto Rican Hawaiian, Blase Camacho Souza, donated her papers after devoting her life to documenting the migration to the Pacific archipelago from 1899-2003. Other West Coast collections arrived at Centro under different circumstances. Writer Aurora Levins Morales, founder and leader of the California Puerto Rican Historical Society's Oral History Project, requested support from our institute to microfilm the records of the oldest Puerto Rican organization in the United States, the Club Puertorriqueño de San Francisco. These collaborations help to illustrate the nature of our work with individuals and organizations, and how archives can benefit from seeking historical documents and resources throughout the United States.

The Centro Archives' contribution to the academic fields of Puerto Rican, Latino and American studies has been important. Material from our archives have been used in scholarly publications (books, journal articles and dissertations), in the development of curricular materials, novels, and posters, and also in exhibitions in collaboration with the Museum of the City of New York, El Museo del Barrio, the New York Historical Society, the Clemente Soto Vélez Cultural and Educational Center, the Smithsonian, and the American University Museum in Washington, DC. We have collaborated in films by WGBH and WETA, and also in documentaries about Puerto Rican and Latino Politics in New York State, Vieques, Puerto Rican migration, Pura Belpré, Frank Bonilla and Clemente Soto Vélez. Recently, in collaboration with the new Hunter College East Harlem Gallery we prepared four gallery exhibits. Statewide collaborations include two New York State Archives digital initiatives, Ventana al Pasado and the Electronic Schoolhouse. In recent years the Centro Archives Historical Preservation and Research Partnership Program has provided support to over twenty research projects in various fields, and the 100 Puerto Ricans: Preserving Our History initiative will expand our collections' scope and breadth.

Legend

Dates of the
collection's
documents

Volume in
cubic feet

Number of
digital objects

Type of search:
description,
inventory
finding aid

A-D

Collection contains the manuscript for a television drama titled *He Can't Even Read Spanish*, as well as a letter to Lillian López, of New York Public Library's South Bronx Project, and some promotional materials and New York Times article for an equivalent WNBC series title *They Can't Even Speak Spanish*.

Topics: Literature; Television

| 📅 1890-1904 | 📦 0.05 | 🧭 1 | 🔍 Description |

The Eddie Aguilar Photographic Collection

CITY OF NEW YORK
HUMAN RESOURCES ADMINISTRATION

Latino Heritage Committee 2000

"Nuestra Cultura Latina es Nuestra Fuerza"
"Our Latin Culture Is Our Strength"

Eddie Aguilar,
Assistant Chair

A photographer who was honored as the Godfather of the Atlantic City Puerto Rican Day Parade in 2005. The collection consists of thousands of prints and negatives of Latino celebrities and musicians including Marc Anthony, Celia Cruz, Tito Puente, Johnny Pacheco, Yomo Toro and many more. His photographs were published in Latin Beat Magazine, puertoricans.com and other publications. He attended almost every major parade in the tri-state area and has pictures of many of them.

Topics: Arts; Architecture and Culture; Family and Community; General

| 📅 1980s-1990s | 📦 10.0 | 🧭 1 | 🔍 Inventory |

The Albors Photographic Collection

The collection consists of 86 photos of the Puerto Rican Day Parade and labor groups photos. Labor groups included are: District 65-Retail Wholesale and Department Store Union, Local 6-Hotel and Club Employees Union, 1199, Local 60-Luggage Workers Union, Labor Committee, International Ladies Garment Workers Union (ILGWU), Club 1380, Isabela Social Club, Migration Division, *El Diario*, Hispanic Auxiliary Police Association, Local 485 and Liga Puerta De Tierra.

Topics: Arts; Music; Culture; Puerto Rican Day Parade; Labor

| 📅 1890-1904 | 📦 0.25 | 🧭 5 | 🔍 Inventory |

Community activist and senior citizen advocate. This a resource for research in grass-roots organizing, community activism, senior citizen life in New York City, particularly in East Harlem and the development of East Harlem. The materials document organizations in which Allende was active, among them Community Board 11, Iris House, the Bonifacio Cora Texidor Housing Development Fund Corporation, the Institute for the Puerto Rican/ Hispanic Elderly, Inc., East Harlem Community Health Committee and the Gran Orden Fraternal de Odfelos Latinos. The bulk of the material is from 1970 to 2001. The materials document cultural and political organizations and contain correspondence, clippings, community newspapers, memorabilia, photographs and presentations.

Topics: Family and Community Life; Social Reform, Gender and Sexuality; Health and Community Welfare

📅 1926-2004   📦 17   ⊘ 17   🔍 Finding Aid

The collection consists of correspondence, song title sheets, music notes, writings, newspaper articles, concert programs, photographs and music CD's of Álvarez.

Topics: Music

📅 1980s-1990s   📦 0.12   ⊘ 8   🔍 Inventory

Andrade has been an active participant in Hispanic labor organizations and held various positions in the Hispanic Labor Committee and the Labor Council for Latin American Advancement. A life-long activist and leader in the labor movement, Andrade first worked as an organizer in Miami and New York after arriving from El Salvador. She was the director of the Department of Education for the International Ladies Garment Workers Union (ILGWU), where she was responsible for worker education programs. The collection consists of correspondence, photographs, event programs, invitations, flyers and pamphlets, mainly about activities in the New York metropolitan area. Her collection is especially rich in photographs of women in union activities.

Topics: Education; Organizations and Leaders

📅 1960s-1980s   📦 8.20   ⊘ 15   🔍 Inventory

Lawyer and civil rights activist. These papers captures the militancy and turbulence of the Puerto Rican independence movement particularly during the 1970s. The papers document the history of leftist movements in Puerto Rico, as well as in the Puerto Rican communities of the United States. Of great significance is the information on the history of the PSP in the United States, where it had a branch and also published a bilingual edition of its newspaper, *Claridad*. Other major themes of the papers are the decolonization of Puerto Rico as an issue before the UN, the Wells Fargo robbery in Hartford and Puerto Rican political prisoners. Types of materials include letters, memoranda, reports, pamphlets and newspaper clippings.

Topics: Politics, Government, and Law; Social Reform

1936-2002   15.69   1   Finding Aid

The Juanita Arocho Papers

Community activist and journalist. Collection contains correspondence, articles, photographs and printed matter pertaining to the participation of Juanita Arocho in the Masons and the movement for the independence of Puerto Rico. The papers provide insight into community organizing efforts in the Puerto Rican community of East (Spanish) Harlem, Puerto Rican independence movements and the participation of Puerto Ricans in the Masonic Order.

Topics: Family and Community; Organization and Leaders; Politics, Government and Law; Social Reform

1940-1994   1.25   17   Finding Aid

The Genoveva de Arteaga Papers

Pianist, organist, teacher and choir director. The collection documents the growth of musical, literary, cultural and civic organizations among Puerto Ricans in New York City. The papers include personal documents, correspondence, flyers, writings, invitations, newspaper clippings, scrapbooks and photographs. The papers, which are primarily in Spanish, contain information about her and her husband, Andrés S. Dalmau, as well as her father Julio C. de Arteaga.

Topics: Arts and Culture; Gender and Sexuality; Music

1910s-1991   12.60   14   Finding Aid

19

The collection comprises more than 1500 items dating from 1940s to the present. The collection includes art works by Puerto Rican artists from the island and from the Diaspora. Highlighted in the collection are art works by Jorge Soto, Manny Vega, Gilberto Hernandez, Papo Colo, Marcos Dimas and Fernando Salicrup. Also represented are works by artists such as Lorenzo Homar, Antonio Martorell, Rafael Tufiño and Jose Rosa. The Collection also contains art prints from art collective like Taller Boricua and Taller Loiza. Included are the portfolios of Los casos de Ignacio, El Cafe, Dos Mundos (photographs), Plena and New York-based Proletario and Taller Boricua. The posters depict soci-cultural as well as political events: including theatre, music dance, film, Comite de Noviembre, Fiesta de San Juan, Fiestas de Loiza and Centro events. Political figures and issues include registration and voting campaigns, Herman Badillo, Nydia Velzquez, Fernando Ferrer and the Young Lords. Overall, the collection contains art prints, photographs and calendars, many of which are limited editions.

Topics: Arts and Culture

📅 1890-1904	📦 0.5	🧭 1	🔍 Description

The Carlos Arroyo Papers

Carlos Arroyo dedicated 20 years of his life to working exclusively as a successful professional dancer. His passion for dance took him all around the world. He collaborated with some of the best Latin and North American musicians of the 1950s and '60s. He is described as one of the greatest Latin rhythm dancers of the period, as evidenced by his collection of documents at the Centro Archives. Despite having "retired" as a dancer to pursue other interests, he reappeared as part of a homage to Tito Puente at Yale University in January 2000 with Mercedes Ellington, Duke Ellington's granddaughter. In 2005, he was recognized by the Pierre Dulaine Dance Club as one of the dance celebrities of the Palladium dance era. The collection consist of photographs, clippings, ephemera, and other documents.

Topics: Arts; Music; Community Life

📅 ca. 1950-1970	📦 0.25	🧭 149	🔍 Inventory

The ASPIRA of New York, Inc., Records

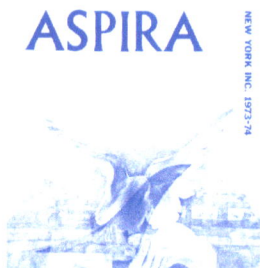

The records document the administration, programs and civic contributions of this groundbreaking social service agency. Furthermore, they help chronicle the organizational evolution of the institution and the numerous initiatives it undertook to support Puerto Rican and Latino youth in New York City. A small but insightful collection, highlights of the records include materials on programs Youth Leadership Development Program, the Office of Research and Advocacy and the ASPIRA Clubs Federation. The collection documents the organization's engagement with current issues in education and politics and its extensive involvement in and influence on decision-making around them. The materials consist of correspondence, memoranda, minutes, photographs, flyers, clippings, proposals, contracts, reports, speeches, videos, slides and financial statements.

Topics: Education; Family and Community Life; Health and Community Welfare; Organizations and Leaders; Social Reform

📅 1959-1998	📦 26.0	🧭 39	🔍 Finding Aid

The materials in the collection span the years from 1944 to 1994. They consist of a small array of personal documents, correspondence, publications, clippings, Masons related materials and organizational ephemera. In addition, the papers contain a strong collection of photographs, particularly of Masonic activities. The folders are arranged alphabetically and the documents are arranged chronologically.

Topics: Family and Community; Organization and Leaders; Politics, Government and Law; Social Reform

📅 1975-2000	📦 0.25	🌀 1	🔍 Inventory

The Asociación de Residentes y Descendientes Puertorriqueños en Cuba Collection

The Cuba/Ricans Project 2003 Collection consists of photographs, forms, a questionnaire, and by-laws of the Asociación de Residentes y Descendientes Puertorriqueños en Cuba, an organization formed to group all of the Puerto Ricans and their descendants who reside permanently in the Republic of Cuba, as well as temporary residents who reside there for employment or academic purposes. Also included in the collection are video cassettes, mini digital video cassettes, and DVR's of interviews with members of this group.

Topics: Migration and Settlemen; Family and Community Life

📅 2003	📦 0.25	🌀 5	🔍 Inventory

Ateneo Puertorriqueño de Nueva York (1962-1987) in The Diana Ramírez de Arellano Papers

Literary organization founded in 1963 by Diana Ramírez de Arellano and other intellectuals "to bridge the gap odf silence and loneliness of the Puerto Rican artist and scholar in New York." The series contains five scrapbooks with all of the records created by the Ateneo such as bylaws, minutes, invitations, press releases, reviews, programs and photographs. The records document how de Arellano and her sister, Daphne, led the organization and presided over its literary programs and conferences. The Ateneo frequently bestowed tributes, and medals of honor upon Puerto Rican artists, writers and intellectuals. The documents consist of letters, minutes, articles, books, programs, newspaper clippings, audiotapes and phonograph records.

Topics: Arts and Culture; Education; Literature; Organizations and Leaders; Gender and Sexuality

📅 1947-1997	📦 3.81	🌀 1	🔍 Finding Aid

Poet who arrived in New York in 1926. For 30 years, he was editor and director of publicity for Hispanoamerica, an important New York film company. Interested in the Hispanic population and culture, he also presided over organizations such as El Círculo de Escritores y Poetas Iberoamericanos (CEPI), which he co-founded, El Instituto de Puerto Rico, la Sociedad Puertorriqueña de Escritores (New York Chapter) and La Fiesta de San Juan Bautista. He was also named Commissioner of the Commission for Human Rights of New York from 1955 to 1966. The collection is arranged by subject and includes newspaper articles, certificates, correspondence, poems, a copy of Aviles' book, personal writings, flyers, publications, photographs and pocket diaries. This collection complements the papers of Diana Ramírez de Arellano, Puerto Rican poet and founder of Ateneo Puertorriqueño of Nueva York, as well as the Felipe N. Torres Papers on Fiesta de San Juan

Topics: Organizations; Education

	ca. 1950-1970		0.25		149		Inventory

The Alfredo Barela Collection

The Alfredo Barela collection consists of 35 photographs of the theatrical actor, including portraits, scenes from performances and cast shots. The photographs are arranged by subject.

Topics: Arts

	ca. 1940s		0.25		5		Inventory

The Efraín Barradas Collection

Professor, Spanish/Latin American Studies, University of Florida, Gainseville. Papers include clippings on literature and theater, correspondence, event programs, articles and a number of books and other publications.

Topics: Arts; Literature

	1959-1998		26.0		39		Inventory

Records of El Barrio Popular Education Program

El Barrio Popular Education Program began in 1985 as a research project of the Language Policy Task Force of the Center for Puerto Rican Studies of The City University of New York. The program's goal was for adult students to develop their reading, writing and computing skills in Spanish while learning English as a Second Language through a participatory methodology. The collection consists of administrative files, minutes, correspondence, photographs, clippings, newsletters and videotapes.

Topics: Education; Social Reform; Organizations; Family and Community

	1985-1990s		25.0		2		Inventory

22

Author, storyteller who wrote and re-interpreted Puerto Rican folk tales and the first Puerto Rican librarian in New York Public Library. These papers are an important source for the study of Puerto Rican children's literature and Puerto Rican folk tales and legends. They are valuable for examining relationships between the Puerto Rican community and a major institution such as the New York Public Library. Additionally, the Papers document the formation and organizational development of the Puerto Rican community in New York City. The materials include personal documents, financial statements from publishers, correspondence, manuscripts, flyers, clippings, photographs and illustrations.

Topics: Arts and Culture; Education; Literature; Family and Community; Social Reform; Gender and Sexuality

📅 1897-1985   📦 18.75   🔘 198   🔍 Finding Aid

The Records of El Bohio Community and Cultural Center, Inc.

El Bohio operated by CHARAS, Inc. as a community and cultural center located in a former Public School in the Lower East Side. El Bohio provided space to a number of community organizations involved in services to youth, fine arts, performing arts, housing assistance and other cultural projects. These organizations in turn provided low-income residents of Loisaida as it is known this Puerto Rican neighborhood with a variety of activities and programs.

Topics: Arts and Culture, Organizations and Leaders

📅 1975-1998   📦 1   🔘   🔍 Description

The papers help document the dynamic career of a key figure in the fields of Puerto Rican Studies, Latin American Studies and Political Science, and first director of the Centro de Estudios Puertorriqueños. Moreover, they chronicle the activities of organizations and governmental initiatives that sought to engage with a number of issues, among them welfare, joblessness, race, minority educational achievement, housing and other social justice issues.

Highlights of the papers include writings by Bonilla on themes ranging in scope from Venezuelan elites to the state of Latino research after the events of 9/11, files on organizations as diverse as the National Jobs For All Coalition, American Friends Service Committee, the Centro de Estudios del Desarrollo, Universidad Central e Venezuela (CENDES) and the Puerto Rican Revolutionary Workers Organization, as well as other materials that document Bonilla's academic career, political activities and life after his retirement from the Centro de Estudios Puertorriqueños in 1993. The materials consists of correspondence, memoranda, photographs, flyers, clippings, writings, remarks, speeches, publications, videotapes and artifacts. The folders are arranged alphabetically and the documents are arranged chronologically.

Topics: Education; Organizations; Leaders

📅 1946-2011   📦 12   🔘 163   🔍 Finding Aid

23

The Joseph A. Burgos Collection

Joseph is the son of José Federico Burgos, who migrated to New York in 1949. He became member of many Puerto Rican cultural organizations in the city, receiving many certificates of merit for his literature and community service. The collection consists of one folder of magazine and newspaper articles belonging to his father, poet and author José Federico Burgos (1921-2001), brother to famous Puerto Rican poet Julia de Burgos.

Topics: Arts and Culture

| 📅 1978-2004 | 📦 0.10 | 🕐 5 | 🔍 Inventory |

The Jose Buscaglia Collection

The collection consists of two folders detailing a proposal for a sculptural plaza to be built in New York City, created by the famous Puerto Rican sculptor and artist, which he presented to Centro in May of 2000 to gain our support for the project. The plaza would contain three allegorical figures representing the three main cultural and ethnic groups that compose Puerto Ricans: Taíno-Arawak, Iberian-Phoenician (Hispanic-Mediterranean) and African. Included in these packets are brief bios, curriculum vitae, images of the artist's work and written proposals.

Topics: Arts; Architecture

| 📅 2000 | 📦 0.05 | 🕐 6 | 🔍 Inventory |

The Buttons Collection

The Buttons Collection consists of over 300 items originally forming part of personal papers or organizational records. Among these are Justo A. Marti, Pura Belpré, José López, Ruth M. Reynolds, Petra Allende, Centro and the National Congress for Puerto Rican Rights. Though the majority of the items are Puerto Rican, the collection also includes other Latinos, particularly Mexican-Chicanos. The buttons are predominantly political in theme, representing elected officials, such as Herman Badillo, or the struggle in Vieques to remove the U.S. Navy from the Island. Many also represent organizations, such as the National Congress for Puerto Rican Rights, ASPIRA and Fiesta Folklorica. A highlight of this collection is items from the José López Papers, which include buttons for the United Farm Workers, the UFW boycott and César Chávez. López was a labor organizer in New York City who was a supporter and participant in the UFW boycott.

Topics: Politics, Culture

| 📅 1930s-1990s | 📦 3 | 🕐 1 | 🔍 Inventory |

24

Educator, community organizer and activist. These papers are important for the information they provide and the insight they offer on the right to equal educational opportunities in the Puerto Rican and Latino community of New York City. Advocacy for bilingual education, community efforts to get Latino representation on the Board of Education of the City of New York and the reform of district boards are all highlighted here. The collection also provides a history of the Puerto Rican/Latino Education Roundtable and perspective on the role Diana Caballero played in civil rights organizations such as the National Congress for Puerto Rican Rights. Materials contained include administrative files such as financial documents, minutes, news clippings, reports, and press releases.

Topics: Education; Family and Community; Organization and Leaders; Gender and Sexuality

| 1967-1999 | 19.72 | 132 | Finding Aid |

The Susanne Cabañas Collection

Poet. Collection consists of two videotapes, one on Anita Vélez Mitchell and the other titled "Momentos Inolvidables de la Familia San Antonio."

Topics: Literature

| 1970s-1980s | 0.50 | 1 | Inventory |

The Gonzalo Cabassa Ramírez Collection

The collection consists of personal documents and correspondence belonging or relating to the Puerto Rican independence supporter and member of the Puerto Rican Nationalist Party, including government documents, such as Cabassa Ramírez's resignation of U.S. citizenship, police and judicial records, intelligence reports, clippings and two military photographs.

Topics: Politics, Government and Law; Social Reform;

| 1953-1999 | 0.12 | 6 | Inventory |

Community Coordinator at New York City Department for the Aging. Elba Cabrera family moved to New York during the Depression, settling in El Barrio and years later moving to the Bronx. Elba worked for over four decades with non-profit organizations, retiring from the Girl Scouts of the USA after 10 years of employment with them. Elba has been active on numerous Boards which include: Hostos Community College Foundation, Bronx Council on the Arts, the Association of Hispanic Arts (AHA), All Care Provider Services; additionally, she is also a member of the Council at Advent Lutheran Church in Manhattan. Her past affiliations as a board member are: Marymount College, ASPIRA, New York Metro Committee UNICEF, New York Women's Agenda and Friends of El Centro de Estudios Puertorriqueños at Hunter College. The collection consists of correspondence, clippings, photographs, event programs, invitations, flyers, pamphlets, posters and videotapes (ranging in theme), a copy of the script for the film "Fort Apache: The Bronx," signed copies of Musica hispana en nuestra vidas/Hispanic Music in Our Lives, Almanaque 1982 Calendar and a photograph.

Topics: Arts; Architecture and Culture; Family and Community; Gender and Sexuality

📅 1970s-1990s	📦 9	🕐 138	🔍 Inventory

California Puerto Rican Historical Society West Coast Oral History Project Collection

Oral History Project documenting 24 interviewees from the West Coast Puerto Rican Elders conducted by the California Puerto Rican Historical Society with funds from the Western Region Puerto Rican Council and Hayward Area Historical Society. Centro provided assistance reformatting audio cassettes into digtial format.

Topics: History; Migration and Settlement

📅 2008	📦 0.05	🕐 6	🔍 Inventory

Boricua-Hawaiana activist and educator. These papers are a significant resource for Puerto Rican migration studies and shed light on the life of plantation laborers in Hawaii in the 1900s and their descendants. The papers provide an intimate portrait of family life and work, as well as the social and cultural networks created by migrants in their efforts to preserve Puerto Rican traditions. The documents include letters, photographs, manuscripts, notes, programs, flyers, newspaper clippings, publications, posters, and artifacts. Included in the papers are letters, manuscripts, notes, programs, flyers, photographs, newspaper clippings and memorabilia.

Topics: Education; Family and Community Life; Migration and Settlement; Organization and Leaders; Gender and Sexuality

📅 1899-2003	📦 13.0	🕐 1,372	🔍 Finding Aid

Collection includes exhibition catalogs and information on Puerto Rican artists living in New York and on the island.

Topic: Art; Culture

📅 1980-2006   📦 .5   🧭 1   🔍 Inventory

The Alice Cardona Papers

Long-time activist Alice Cardona is best known for her commitment to advocacy for bilingual education, women's rights and political representation. She worked and volunteered for ASPIRA, the National Conference of Puerto Rican Women, the Puerto Rican/Latino Education Roundtable and the Puerto Rican Association for Community Affairs and the National Latinas Caucus. From 1983-1995 as the assistant director of the New York State Division for Women, she supported numerous initiatives and community-based groups. The papers document the bilingual education movement in New York City, as well as the development of organizations that served the needs of women and those oriented toward community development. Materials consist of biographical information; correspondence; news clippings; photographs; speeches; articles; and documents from various organizations, including regulations, programs, correspondence and meeting minutes. The collection contains a significant number of news clippings and other biographical materials; there are also subject files, audiovisual materials and photographs.

Topics: Education: Education; Organizations and Leaders; Politica; Government and Reform; Social Reform

📅 1923-2001   📦 34   🧭 36   🔍 Finding Aid

The Luis A. Cardona Oral History Collection

Louis Cardona was an officer of the Migration Division of the Offices of the Government of Puerto Rico in the U.S. The Louis Cardona collection consists of 37 audiocassette interviews of community leaders dating circa early 1980s.

Topics: Migration and Settlement

📅 1980s   📦 0.5   🧭 1   🔍 Inventory

Caribbean Cultural Center Photographs

The collection consists of photographs of Taino Indians and African art, and early images of Puerto Rico. Many of the photographs are by Hiram Maristany. These images were exhibited in the Caribbean Cultural Center gallery.

Topics: Visual Arts; Culture; History

📅 1980s   📦 2   🧭 0   🔍 Inventory

The John Carro Collection

The collection consists of various documents on the Puerto Rican and Hispanic Leadership Forum, including newspaper articles, correspondence, writings and reports donated by Judge John Carro, a member of the Forum's Executive Committee.

Topics: Organization and Leaders; Politics, Government and Law

| 📅 1958-1994 | 📦 1.0 | 🕐 7 | 🔍 Inventory |

The Rudy Castilla Photographs Collection

The collection is a photograph collection of Puerto Rican and other Hispanic entertainers, performers and celebrities taken by the famed Castilla Photo studio in East Harlem (El Barrio), New York. Many prints from this period were destroyed when the studio underwent changes in ownership. There are also miscellaneous items, such as postcards of Puerto Rico.

Topics: Community Life; Culture

| 📅 1890-1904 | 📦 0.4 | 🕐 7 | 🔍 Inventory |

Centro de Estudios Puertorriqueños Records (CENTRO)

The only research center devoted to the study of the Puerto Rican diaspora. The records document the founding, administration, programs and intellectual production of this pioneering and innovative institution. In addition, the collection attests to Centro's role within the Puerto Rican/Latino community, its influence in academic circles and its ongoing commitment to chronicling and interpreting the Puerto Rican experience in the United States. An extraordinarily rich collection, highlights of the records include materials on the origins of Centro, its alternative modes of internal governance, the numerous projects and initiatives undertaken by its research task forces and units and the multiple organizations staff helped establish and/or actively participated in. The collection chronicles institutional efforts to document, through writings, archival initiatives, oral history interviews, publications and film, the history, culture, and social, civic and political contributions of the Puerto Rican community to contemporary American life. Records include correspondence, memoranda, minutes, photographs, flyers, clippings, proposals, reports, speeches, videos, slides, financial statements and artifacts. New Additions include: Félix Matos Rodríguez (Centro Director), Camille Rodriguez (Administrator and researcher in the Higher Education Task Force, Blanca Vázquez (Centro Bulletin editor), Pedro Pedraza (Language Task Force), Susan Zeig Film and Media, The Library Vertical Files, Slide Collection, CENTRO/LEMC audio, video and transcripts files.

Topics: Culture; Education; Organizations and Leaders; Health and Community Welfare; Social Reform

| 📅 1973-2013 | 📦 135.0 | 🕐 182 | 🔍 Finding Aid |

Josefina Cintrón Collection

The collection consists of various personal documents, including certificates, newspaper articles, clippings, programs and correspondence relating to cultural and literary organizations, including Instituto de Puerto Rico of New York and El Círculo de Escritores y Poetas Iberoamericanos (CEPI).

Topics: Arts; Culture; Organizations

1926-2004	17.0	17	Inventory

The Records of CHARAS

Founded in the 1960s as "The Real Great Society, Inc.," by Chino Garcia, Armando Perez, Bimbo Rivas, Alfredo Irizarry and Roberto Nazario. To help catalyze the revitalization of the surrounding "Loisaida." Collections contains records, correspondence and art materials.

Topics: Community Life; Arts

1960-2008	25.0	76	Inventory

The Claridad Bilingüe Collection, 1971-1985

This collection is made up of thousands of photographic negatives intended for use in the pages of the bilingual edition of the leftist Puerto Rican newspaper, *Claridad*.

Topics: Politics, Government and Law; Social Reform

1967-1980	2.0	5	Description

The Club Puertorriqueño de San Francisco Minutes

The oldest Puerto Rican community organization stateside. Originally founded with the intention to represent Puerto Rico in the Panama Pacific International Exposition in San Francisco in 1915. The organization received the remaining funds of La Sociedad Puertorriqueña de Beneficiencia Mutua, 1907 to 1915. The minutes are all in Spanish, but as early as 1927 there is discussion of allowing members to speak in English at general assemblies since some members were not born on the island. In 1932, the Club discussed offering membership to women, and in fact, they even rented out their space to Las Puerto Rican Daughters to host a dance. By 1934, there are female members, who paid special (lower) membership dues. Collection consists of 2 microfilm reels.

Topics: Migration and Settlemen; Family and Community Life

1915-1969	0.1	1	Description

Political activist, feminist and writer. Resource for examining the Communist Party of the United States and the independence movement of Puerto Rico as well as political persecution, feminism and trade-unionism. Collection consists of manuscripts, notes, letters, press releases, programs, flyers and newspapers clippings.

Topics: Politics, Government, and Law; Social Reform; Gender and Sexuality

| 📅 1932-1970 | 📦 1.44 | 🧭 17 | 🔍 Finding Aid |

The Jesús Colón Papers

Pioneeer, community leader, labor organizer and a prolific writer. The Papers are a significant contribution to the study of Puerto Rican history and especially to the reconstruction of Puerto Rican community history in New York. They support research on such topics as organizational development and political participation among Puerto Ricans in New York, employment, discrimination and the labor movement. The Puerto Rican involvement in labor and left organizations in New York are documented. In the collection there are letters, notes, drafts of published and unpublished works, reports, clippings and photographs. A majority of the papers consisting of organizational records such as by-laws, lists, programs and policy statements.

Topics: Organization and Leaders; Migration and Settlement; Family and Community Life; Politics; Social Reform; Gender and Sexuality

| 📅 1901-1974 | 📦 25.5 | 🧭 773 | 🔍 Finding Aid |

Joaquín Colón López

Joaquín Colón López was a Puerto Rican activist and writer, brother to writer Jesús Colón. He also co-founded Club Democrático de Brooklyn with J.V. Alonso. The collection consists of documents and 262 photographs dating from 1917 to 1947. Included among the documents are biographical information, articles, and a typewritten manuscript of Colón López's book, *Pioneros Puertorriqueños en Nueva York 1917-1947*. This manuscript was submitted by Centro and published by Arte Público Press in 2001. The photographs include personal and family photos as well as political activities and events.

Topics: Community Life; Migration and Settlement; Social Reform

| 📅 1917-1947 | 📦 0.50 | 🧭 9 | 🔍 Inventory |

The Máximo Cólon Photographic Collection

Photographer. Collection includes photographs, buttons, posters and clippings. The papers demonstrate Colón's work in as a photographer and activities in the Puerto Rican community and focus mainly on New York City.

Topics: Community Life

| 📅 1960s-1980s | 📦 0.30 | 🧭 7 | 🔍 Inventory |

The Miriam Colón Collection

Miriam Colón

Actor and Founder of the Puerto Rican Traveling Theater. Colón was born and raised in Ponce, Puerto Rico. She studied at the University of Puerto Rico, where she received a scholarship to study at the Dramatic Workshop and Technical Institute in New York. Miriam currently serves as the artistic director of the Puerto Rican Traveling Theater, which she founded in 1969. Colón became one of the first Puerto Rican actors to become a great success in Hollywood, starring in many films alongside such famed actors as Marlon Brando. She has also appeared on Broadway and off-Broadway productions. The collection consists of personal and biographical information, correspondence, programs, and clippings on Colón and the Puerto Rican Traveling.

Topics: Arts; Culture

📅 1953-1987   📦 0.25   💿 8   🔍 Inventory

The Ramón Colón Papers

Ramón Colón was a Puerto Rican politician, member of the Republican Party. He was brother-in-law to distinguished writers Jesús and Joaquín Colón. This collection includes an invitation to the inauguration of President Eisenhower, 21 photographs of political meetings and events, an event booklet signed by Ramón Colón containing a list of members and supporters of the club and a publication entitled "El Estado Puerto Rico," endorsing statehood for Puerto Rico.

Topics: Politics, Government, and Law

📅 1950s-1960s   📦 0.25   💿 5   🔍 Inventory

The Yarisa Colón Art Books Collection

Poet. Collection of several art books donated by Yarisa Colón Included are some of her works such as *Desvestida* (2001), and others created in collaboration with Tanya Torres like *Imágenes femeninas* (2002)

Topics: Arts and Culture, Organizations and Leaders

📅 2001-2005   📦 0   💿 0   🔍 Description

The Gilberto Concepción de Gracia New York Years Collection

Collection consists of digitized documents and photographs. Founder and President of the Puerto Rican Independence Party (PIP), Concepción de Gracia is an outstanding figure in Puerto Rican political history. He passionately argued for Puerto Rico's independence and for social justice for all Puerto Ricans. He was also a distinguished lawyer, journalist and professor. In 1936 he moved to the United States where he fought, first in New York City and later in Washington D.C., for the rights of Puerto Ricans and their communities. As a Senator (1952 to 1960) in the Puerto Rican parliament, he introduced key progressive legislation on social, political and cultural issues. He presided over the Puerto Rican Bar Associations' Civil Liberties Commission and appeared before the United Nations on the question of Puerto Rico. A firm believer in democracy, Concepción de Gracia fought tirelessly until his death for the Puerto Rican Independence Party to remain as an instrument to attain national sovereignty. Inventory available

Topics: Migration and Settlement, Politics, Community Life

📅 1936-1939   📦 0.25   💿 139   🔍 Inventory

Collection consists of three family photographs from early 1930s.

Topics: Family and Community Life

| 1930s | 0.01 | 1 | Inventory |

The Joe Conzo Collection

Photographer. Born and raised in the South Bronx growing up around his grandmother, the dynamic South Bronx leader and activist Dr. Evelina López Antonetty and his father, long time confidant and historian of the late Tito Puente, Joe Conzo, Sr., Conzo's photographic work was deeply influenced by a strong legacy of Puerto Rican activism in the South Bronx, as well as the vibrancy of Puerto Rican musical culture in New York. Conzo photographed street parties, concerts, and other gatherings that reflected the innovations in dance, music and fashion that Hip Hop brought to the fore. In addition, he was an astute chronicler of the social and physical context from which Hip Hop arose, with his work including poignant and captivating images of the devastated urban landscape of the South Bronx, as well as the surrounding Puerto Rican community. The collection consists of five photographs donation representing his scope of work as presented in The Bronx: Mi Barrio, Mi Orgullo Photography by Joe Conzo exhibited in the Centro Gallery in 2010. Inventory available.

Topics: Visual Arts; Photography

| 1979-1981 | 0.05 | 47 | Inventory |

The Félix L. Cordero Meléndez Collection

Félix Cordero Meléndez is a photographer and painter who studied in New York City and Chicago. In 1984, he received the Artist of the Year Award from the Institute of Puerto Rico in New York. The Félix Cordero Meléndez collection consists of biographical information, slides of photographs, descriptive information, exhibit programs, and two photographs dating 1992.

Topics: Arts

| 1980s-1994 | 0.25 | 5 | Inventory |

The Félix Cordero Collection

Painter. Collection comprises one legal size folder and includes slides, exhibition catalogues and information, pamphlets and a postcard.

Topics: Visual Arts

| 1981-1986 | 0.05 | 7 | Inventory |

The María Cortijo Collection

A resident of Brooklyn since the 1950's, Cortijo is a Puerto Rican artist who created an art form, weaving dolls and other artifacts, such as handbags, baskets and even vests from disposable plastic bags. The María Cortijo collection consists of biographical information, a photograph, and a woven vest.

Topics: Arts

| 📅 2002 | 📦 0.12 | 💿 6 | 🔍 Inventory |

The Marithelma Costa Interviews Collection

Modern Latin America Literature Professor at Hunter College, CUNY. This collection is comprised of 10 audiocassettes with interviews with the poets Clemente Soto Vélez and Carmen Valle, scholar and essayist Nilita Vientos Gastón and the visual artist and essayist Antonio Martorell.

Topics: Culture; Literature

| 📅 1985-1986 | 📦 0.10 | 💿 1 | 🔍 Inventory |

Cuatro Project Collection

The Cuatro Project is a cultural organization that focuses on the history of the cuatro, a traditional Puerto Rican stringed musical instrument, and its relationship to Puerto Ricans. Group dedicated to discovering the history of the cuatro and its links to Puerto Rican identity.

Topics: Music; Culture

| 📅 1991-1998 | 📦 0.12 | 💿 7 | 🔍 Description |

The Pura Cruz Collection

Cruz arrived in New York as an infant and grew up in East Harlem (El Barrio), New York. She studied studio art at SUNY at Stonybrook and went on to become a visual artist, sculptor and curator. Her style is expressionist, somewhat abstract, large-scale, and employs mixed media. Her works often deal with such themes as ethnic identity and memory. The collection consists of 40 slides of artwork, clippings and exhibit program facsimiles donated by the artist.

Topics: Art

PURA
CRUZ

| 📅 1983-1992 | 📦 0.25 | 💿 6 | 🔍 Inventory |

33

The CUNY Association of Caribbean Studies (CUNYACS) was founded in 1984 among Caribbeanists within the CUNY system and beyond to promote the field of Caribbean Studies and develop a mutual support network. The CUNY Association of Caribbean Studies collection consists of documents, including correspondence, bulletins, newsletters, reports, meeting minutes, memoranda and conference programs.

Topics: Education; Culture

📅 1985-1986   📦 0.25   🕙 5   🔍 Inventory

The Edgar de Jesús Papers

Former assistant manager and director of organizing for the NY/NJ Regional Joint Board of the Union of Needle trades and Textile Employees (UNITE), de Jesús was also a member of the New York City Hispanic Labor Committee, the AFL-CIO Labor Council on Latin American Advancement, the Young Lords/Puerto Rican Revolutionary Workers Organization and the National Congress for Puerto Rican Rights. Collection consists of newsletters, biographies and reports. It deals mainly with activities in the New York metropolitan area.

Topics: Labor and Occupation; Social Reform

📅 1970-2001   📦 0.4   🕙 7   🔍 Inventory

The Ramón Delgado Papers

Ramón Delgado Ramos was a judge and notary public, as well as a poet, writer and musician from San Juan, Puerto Rico. The collection includes original sheet music and lyrics by Ramos, photographs, autographed photographs, lyrics, certificates, a promotional movie booklet for the film *Solomon and Sheba*, and six small books, including an epistolary memoir, essays on religion, spiritualism and metaphysics, and a an issue of *Puerto Rico Ilustrado* dated May 1940.

Topics: Music: Religion

📅 2002   📦 0.12   🕙 10   🔍 Inventory

The Efraín Díaz Santiago Iglesias Educational Society Collection

The Santiago Iglesias Educational Society was formed by members of labor unions from various industries. These included the New York City Central Labor Council, the AFL-CIO, and the International Brotherhood of Electrical Workers Local Union #3, to address the needs and concerns of Puerto Rican and other Hispanic workers and communities in the United States. The collection consists of documents such as personal and biographical information, organization constitution, correspondence, flyers, programs, certificates, photos and clippings, meeting minutes and agendas, and course descriptions relating to the society, its members and its activities. This collection complements other Santiago Iglesias Hispanic Educational Society collections.

Topics: Labor

📅 1958-1996   📦 0.25   🕙 6   🔍 Inventory

The Manuel Diaz Papers

Social worker, activist, and academic. A founding member of such community based organizations as the Puerto Rican Forum, ASPIRA, the Hispanic Youth Association, the Puerto Rican Family Institute and Boricua College, Manuel Díaz trained as a social worker and went on to lead numerous institutions and initiatives, among them the Puerto Rican Community Development Project, Mobilization for Youth and PROGRESS, Inc. He served on the faculties of Columbia University, Boricua College and Fordham University. The papers contain significant material on the life and work of the Puerto Rican social worker and community organizer. His oral autobiography is preserved on a series of audio cassettes, as well as recordings of his academic study, travels and community work. Writings by Díaz detail his life and his outlook on the issues of his time.

Topics: Organization and Leaders; Family and Community Life; Politics; Social Reform; Gender and Sexuality

| 1940-2007 | 7.50 | 8 | Finding Aid |

The William Díaz Papers

The first Latino Program Director for the Ford Foundation (1983) and a Senior Fellow at the University of Minnesota's Hubert H. Humphrey Institute of Public Affairs, William Díaz was also vice chairman of the Minnesota State Latino Affairs Council and helped found the Puerto Rico Community Foundation. He also served on the boards of Hispanics in Philanthropy, Aspira of America and Aspira of New York, Inc. and the Council on Foundations, among other organizations.Collection contains correspondence, speeches, reports, brochures, resumes, newspaper clippings and event programs. The papers span various geographic regions, including New York, Minnesota, Wisconsin and Maryland.

Topics: Labor

| 1980-2001 | 5.0 | 9 | Inventory |

The Doval Family Collection

The Papers are a genealogical collection consisting of seven family portraits and personal documents, such as identification and a copy of a passenger list booklet for the New York and Porto Rico Steamship Company.

Topics: Family and Community Life

| 1914-2000 | 0.15 | 6 | Inventory |

35

E-G

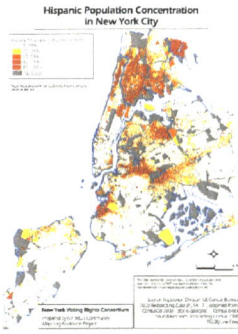

Hispanic Population Concentration in New York City

A civic, non-partisan association committed to the political education and empowerment of the residents of East Harlem, EHCG sought to increase awareness of issues that affected the community and to cultivate leadership amongst its members. Through educational forums, town hall meetings and workshops, the group's intention was, according to its mission statement, to "make the people of East Harlem a positive force in shaping the political decisions that affect their lives." Collection includes agendas, maps, a guidebook and member listings.

Topics: Education; Health and Community Welfare; Community Life

2001-2003   1.25   5   Inventory

East Harlem Council for Community Improvement Inc., Records

Founded in 1979 by residents and community leaders in East Harlem, EHCCI focused on the delivery of a broad range of human services to the residents of Manhattan's Community Planning Board #11. It later expanded its reach and provided services in communities in the South Bronx, Lower East Side and Central and West Harlem.

Topics: Health and Community Welfare

1995-1997   0.25   5   Description

EHCCI
EAST HARLEM COUNCIL FOR COMMUNITY IMPROVEMENT INC.
Programs
Services & Activities

The Diego Echevarría Audiovisual Collection

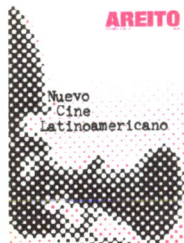

AREITO
Nuevo Cine Latinoamericano

Filmmaker and communications specialist. Collection contains videocassettes, film reels, mixed audio tracks and a number of publications. This collection concerns the PBS Latino-focused program, *Visiones*, and footage about *Los Sures*, his 1984 film documentary about five different people who live in this Brooklyn neighborhood.

Topics: Media, TV

1980s   6.0   1   Description

The Sandra Esteves Collection

Award-winning poet, visual artist and founding member of the Nuyorican poetry movement. Of mixed Puerto Rican and Dominican descent, Sandra Esteves became the first Nuyorican woman to publish a volume of poetry in the United States. The collection includes poems and short stories.

Topics: Arts; Literature

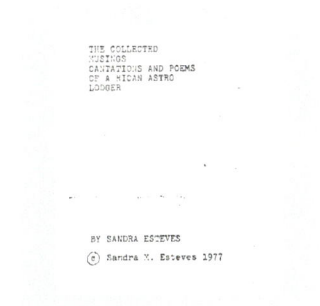

THE COLLECTED
MUSINGS
CANTATIONS AND POEMS
OF A RICAN ASTRO
LOGGER

BY SANDRA ESTEVES
© Sandra M. Esteves 1977

1973-1977   0.05   5   Inventory

Aníbal Félix originally migrated to New York from Santurce, Puerto Rico, in the late 1940s and was a lifelong resident of East Harlem. During the 1950s, he was a music promoter and spent the rest of his working life at Metropolitan Hospital, eventually becoming union representative and shop steward. He was an avid Latin music collector and baseball enthusiast. His papers consist mainly of LP's and audiocassettes documenting Cuban and Puerto Rican music, particularly rare recordings of trios.

Topics: Music; Arts; Recreation; Community Life

1940-1980s   20.0   7   Description

The Fernando Ferrer Electoral Campaign Collection

New York City Council member from 1982-1987, Bronx Borough President from 1987-2001, Ferrer made two bids for Mayoral office in 2001 and 2005. He was a member of ASPIRA in the late 1960s and served as vice-president of the citywide ASPIRA Clubs Federation. Collection includes DVD's, awards, newspapers, audiocassettes, photographs and reports.

Topics: Politics

1988-2005   8.0   25   Inventory

The Víctor Fragoso Collection

Author, playwriter, academic and poet on gay themes. He collaborated with the Puerto Rican Traveling Theater and the Center for Puerto Rican Studies in cultural projects geared toward the Puerto Rican community. Collectiob

Topics: Literature; Poetry

1968-1981   0.1   1   Inventory

The Fragoza Family Collection

The Fragoza collection documents the family participation with the American Legion, Borinquen Post 1216, baseball teams and inside and outside the views of their new residence in the Bronx in the early 1940s.

Topics: Family Life; Community: Migration and settlement

1940's   0.5   17   Inventory

38

OSCAR GARCIA RIVERA
N. Y. State Assemblyman 1937

Politician, lawyer, community activist. First Puerto Rican elected to public office in the U.S. An important source for study of early Puerto Rican political life and of the existent conditions of the East (Spanish) Harlem community in the first part of the twentieth century. In addition, it provides a viewfinder into labor politics and the political and social alliances created among the emerging ethnic communities in NY City. The materials in the collection consist of personal documents, correspondence, photographs, politically related handbills, flyers and other ephemera, clippings and artifacts related to García Rivera's political campaigns.

Topics: Community Welfare; Organizations and Leaders; Politics, Government, and Law; Social Reform

📅 1912-1988   📦 3.0   🔶 77   🔍 Finding Aid

Member of the NY State Assembly (1965 to 1967), the NY State Senate (1967 to 1978), and represented the South Bronx in the U.S. House of Representatives (1978 to 1990). He was the first New York-born Puerto Rican to serve in the U.S. Congress. This collection documents Garcia's work in Congress as NY Representative of the South Bronx. The papers chronicle his work on the Post Office and Civil Service Committee, the Banking, Finance, and Urban Affairs Committee and the Foreign Affairs Committee; and his legislative work on issues of interest, such as immigration reform, bilingual education and teen pregnancy. The collection also contains administrative files from Garcia's Bronx and Washington offices, some personal and biographical information, records pertaining to his reelection campaigns, public relations materials and subject files. Materials are largely textual, comprised of correspondence, memoranda, speeches, statements, financial and legal documents, congressional bills, minutes, agendas, clippings, publications, ephemera, photographs, artifacts, and audio and video recordings.

Topics: Organizations and Leaders; Polititics; Government and Reform

📅 1976-1989   📦 63.0   🔶 8   🔍 Finding Aid

Painter. Collection includes eight posters and several flyers that feature Garcia's realist paintings of scenes from both Puerto Rico and New York City. Included as well are exhibition catalogs.

Topics: Painting; Arts

📅 1990s   📦 1.0   🔶 13   🔍 Inventory

Performance poet, writer and musician. Sandra García-Rivera's collection is made up of poetry, writings, programs, clippings, flyers, photographs, postcards and other ephemera.

Topics: Arts; Literature

📅 1990s-2000   📦 2.0   🔶 10   🔍 Inventory

39

Pioneer and Community Leader. Gerena Valentín is a Puerto Rican pioneer in NY City who also was a key figure in developing major Puerto Rican organizations in New York City between the 1940s to the 1970s. He played a key role in the mobilization of Puerto Ricans in the 1963 and 1968 marches in D.C. as well as the 1964 school boycott in NY City, the largest in the history of the United States. He also served as director of the City Commission of Human Rights and as a City Councilman   representing Council District 11 in the Bronx. Gerena was an active player in the   founding and development the Council of Hometown Clubs, the National Puerto Rican Day Parade, the National Association of Puerto Rican Civil Rights, the Puerto Rican Folkloric   Festival, and the Puerto Rican Community Development Program.

Topics: Politics, Government, and Law; Social Reform

1940s-1970s	Collection promised to Centro	1	Description

The Ruth Glasser Musicians Interview Collection

This collection consists of 40 audiocassette interviews, conducted by Glasser while writing her book/dissertation, *My Music is My Flag*, of Bobby Capó, Johnny Rodríguez, Victoria Hernández, sister to composer Rafael Hernández and owner of Almacenes Hernández in East Harlem, possibly the first Puerto Rican-owned music store in New York City.

Topics: Music and Musicians

1988-1983	2.0	1	Inventory

The Enrique Gómez Collection

Gómez is an actor who has worked with the PR Traveling Theater. The collection consists of slides of PR and Hispanic Day Parades, personal slides, and information and programs on the PR Traveling Theater. The collection complements the Justo A. Martí collection and others which document the evolution of the parades.

Topics: Community Life; Theatre

1971-2000	0.15	5	Inventory

The Carmen González Papers

Social columnist. She published some of her writings in local newspapers such as *El Diario La Prensa* in New York City and in Tampa, Florida. The collection contains photographs and newspaper clippings.

Topics: Culture, Recreation and Leisure

1930-1996	1.0	3	Inventory

Labor organizer and leader. His papers document his lifelong commitment and contributions to Puerto Rican/Latino labor organizing and his role as community organizer for the Migration Division of the Commonwealth of PR. His papers complement also the papers of his wife, Helen Rodríguez Trías.

Topics: Labor and Occupation, Organizations and Leaders, Social Reform

📅 1960s - 2006   📦 15.0   ⏱ 217   🔍 Inventory

Social activist and journalist, as well as a community organizer and labor leader. The papers contain material on the birth and development of several critical Puerto Rican and Latin American organizations, including the National Congress of Puerto Rican Rights, the Alianza Puertorriqueña, the National Association of Hispanic Journalists, and the Young Lords Party. It also contains extensive journalistic material from the author's entire career, as well as source material and correspondence, administrative and organizational material, clippings, correspondence, notes, manuscripts and pamphlets, flyers, photographs, audio and visual files and a small oversize collection.

Topics: Organizations and Leaders; Politics; Government and Law; Social Reform; Labor and Occupation

📅 1945-2012   📦 19.0   ⏱ 8   🔍 Finding Aid

41

H-J

The Jaime Haslip-Peña Collection

Jaime Haslip Peña was born in San Juan, Puerto Rico, and he migrated to New York. He worked on the steamship Borinquen from 1933 to 1941 and for the U.S. Customs Service from 1943 to 1985, during which time he wrote several reports and policy statements. The collection consists of biographical information and photographs. It serves as a documentation of the lives of the steamship merchant marines.

Topics: Business; Commerce; Occupation and Labor

📅 1918-1951   📦 0.12   🕐 6   🔍 Inventory

The Víctor Hernández Cruz Collection

Víctor Hernández Cruz, born in Puerto Rico, moved to the United States in 1954 with his family. He attended high school in New York. Hernández Cruz is a co-founder of both the East Harlem Gut Theatre in New York and the Before Columbus Foundation and a former editor of *Umbra Magazine*. He has taught at the University of California at Berkeley and San Diego, San Francisco State College and the University of Michigan. The collection consist of literary works.

Topics: Arts; Culture

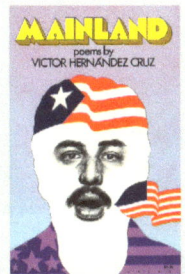

📅 1966-1973   📦 0.05   🕐 5   🔍 Inventory

The Juan Hernández Cruz Collection

Juan Hernández Cruz was an activist and organizer of el Partido Independentista Puertorriqueño, chapter in New York City. He was one of the main spokespersons for the organization in the United Nations Decolonization Committee. This collection documents the independence group's efforts to keep Puerto Rico on the UN Committee agenda after the United States succeeded in removing it from its list of colonial territories in 1952. The collection consists of documents, such as agendas, memorandum, correspondence, bulletins, press releases, reports, speeches, clippings, notes and poems, as well as a political book.

Topics: Organizations and Leaders, Social Reform; Politics, Government, and Law

📅 1958-1982   📦 0.25   🕐 5   🔍 Inventory

The Julio Hernández-Delgado Interviews About the Life of Pura Belpré Collection

The collection consists of 13 audiocassette recordings about author and librarian Pura Belpré's contribution and legacy. Among them are interviews and book readings, several with the children's books writer, Pura Belpré. This collection complements the Pura Belpré Papers, as well as Centro's Oral History Collection by Lillian López.

Topics: Arts; Culture; Literature; Librarianship

📅 1972-1989   📦 0.30   🕐 5   🔍 Inventory

Hernández Álvarez was a consultant with the Ford Foundation in Brazil and Professor at the University of Arizona, Tucson; the University of Wisconsin, Milwaukee; and Hunter College, NY. He also had an early role in the 1980 Census Advisory Committee and worked at the International Population and Urban Research Institute at the University of California, Berkeley. The collection consists of correspondence, photographs, reports, clippings, and postcards. It explores the many facets of Hernández's personal and professional life. It concerns his activities in New York, Milwaukee, Wisconsin, Chicago, Illinois, Brazil and Berkeley, California.

Topics: Education; Gender and Sexuality

| 1952-2006 | 10.0 | 61 | Inventory |

The Pedro Juan Hernández Ephemera Collection

Collection consists of flyers, postcards, playbills, programs, photographs of Puerto Rican neighborhoods in NY City, Chicago and Boston and events such as Puerto Rican Day Parade, posters and other ephemera.

Topics: Community Life; Culture

| 1995-2010 | 2.0 | 5 | Description |

Historical Journals and Periodicals Collection

Collection consists of items from several American publications documenting the Spanish-American War in 1898, the U.S. occupation of Puerto Rico and the period of transition of Puerto Rico from a Spanish colony to U.S. territory. It includes newspapers, magazines, booklets, illustrations, lithographs, postcards and prints; form issues of Harper's Weekly, Leslie's Weekly, Scientific American, Puck, Judge and others. The publications are political in theme, containing articles on key battles in the War and brief biographies on military figures; others were intended to attract tourists to the Puerto Rico, the "newest possession" of the U.S., displaying stunning landscapes and attractions. The publications document the changing attitudes of America toward the Caribbean throughout this time period; therefore, an imperialistic, sometimes racist, ideology is reflected in many of the articles and political cartoons. One highlight of this collection is its impressive artwork, including photographs, cartoons, drawings and sketches from life by well-known artists of the time period.

Topics: Politics

| 1890-1904 | over 100 items | 21 | Inventory |

The Hispanic Ministry collection consists of writings from various church organizations of denominations such as Episcopalian, Baptist, Methodist and Pentecostal, including contact information for the churches and members, as well as writings on language, ethnicity, cultural and socio-economic differences within the church, and various writings on Hispanic congregations.

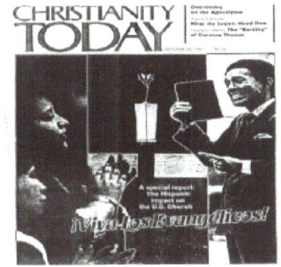

Topics: Religion; Community Life

📅 1951-1991   📦 0.12   🔴 5   🔍 Inventory

The Hispanic Labor Project Collections°

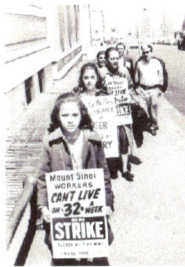

The Labor Project (Hispanic Labor Collection) includes a wide variety of labor leaders and organization collections and document the organizational efforts of the Hispanic community to address the needs and concerns of its workers and communities in the US. It consists of documents and photographs, including union manuals, constitutions, newsletters, event flyers, meeting agendas, correspondence and memos, journal articles, research papers and reports, conference programs, voter registration campaigns, biographical/historical information, and interview transcripts from organizations such as the Hispanic Labor Committee, Labor Council for Latin American Advancement, NY State Dept. of Labor, United Federation of Teachers (Local 2), NY Health and Human Services Union (Local 1199) and the International Ladies Garment Union (Local 62-32).

Topics: Labor and Occupation

📅 1920-2005   📦 1.0   🔴 19   🔍 Inventory

The Records of HoMoVisiones

Cable television program dedicated to gay Latino issues. The collection is made up of correspondence, subject files, organizational files, administrative files, clippings, flyers, posters, proposals, scripts, reports and multi-format videos offering rich documentation on gay, lesbian and Latino social and political movements, as well as their cultural counterparts. It mainly deals with activities in the New York metropolitan area.

Topics: Family and Community; Social Reform; General; Gender and Sexuality

📅 1980-2002   📦 21.0   🔴 57   🔍 Inventory

This event is being videotaped

HV

HoMoVISIONES

The Institute for Puerto Rican/Hispanic Elderly Collection

Founded in 1979 in NY City, the Institute is a non-profit organization with the mission to improve the quality of life of the Puerto Rican/Hispanic elderly, a rapidly growing and diverse population. The collection consists of documents on the institution, including fact sheets, information on services, conference materials, health care pamphlets, an issue of *El Pregonero*, the institute's newspaper, and a pamphlet on scams that was printed by the local government.

Topics: Community Life

📅 1990s   📦 0.15   🔴 5   🔍 Inventory

45

A La Izquierda: The Puerto Rican Movement Collection is an extensive microfilm collection documenting left-wing social movements for justice, independence and human rights in Puerto Rico and the United States during the twentieth century. The collection consists periodicals, newsletters, pamphlets, and other documents representing multiple organizations and individuals that advocated for PR independence and around issues of labor, feminism and human rights issues on the island and in the United States. Represented in this collection are documents originating in Puerto Rico as well as from communities in New York, Chicago, Hartford and California. Also included are materials that document the participation of progressive religious organizations in the cause of independence and social justice as well as other groups that were in solidarity with these causes internationally. This collection provides rich material for researchers and can serve as an introduction into the complex history of the organizations and movements that composed the Puerto Rican left/independence struggle. In many cases, there is no other source of documentation for these groups. The collection contains 20 microfilm reels.

Topics: Politics; Social Reform

| 1923-2002 | 10.0 | 61 | Finding Aid |

The Joffre-Sureda Family Scrapbook

The Joffre-Sureda Family was a middle-class family from Mayagüez, PR that migrated to New York and New Jersey. The scrapbook includes family photographs, mostly of herself and her son, Pedro Antonio, clippings, flyers, invitations and greeting cards, correspondence and other mementos.

Topics: Migration and Settlement; Family

| 1930s | 0.30 | 227 | Inventory |

The Julia Jorge Rosario Papers

Julia Jorge (1935-) has devoted most of her life to the labor movement and union activities. Jorge remains an active member of the Labor Council for Latin American Advancement and the Hispanic Labor Committee. Her papers contain photographs, clippings and newsletters, among other items.

Topics: Labor; Gender and Sexuality

| 1960s-2000 | 10.0 | 43 | Inventory |

L-M

La Luz is a longtime social activist of the Hispanic community and a specialist in labor education programs for the Hispanic trade unionists at the School of Labor and Industrial Relations of Michigan State University. He was also the Socialist Party Chairman in Connecticut. The collection consists of documents, including writings by La Luz and his involvement in the trial of José Torres Cruz and José A. Torres Vega, as well as correspondence, newspaper articles and miscellaneous bulletins, reports and conference materials.

Topics: Labor and Occupation; Social Reform

📅 1971-1991	📦 0.25	🔴 5	🔍 Inventory

Collection contains 32 buttons chronicling the Puerto Rican left, as well as a number of posters. Also included are a series of stamps dating from Puerto Rico's Spanish colonial period, two cloth Puerto Rican flags, numerous posters that document the Puerto Rican left and El Museo del Barrio, as well as calendars and instruction materials that review Puerto Rican history.

Topics: Education; Culture; Politics

📅 1980s	📦 0.75	🔴 5	🔍 Inventory

National Convention of Puerto Rican Women (NACOPRW) promotes the equal participation of Puerto Rican/Hispanic women in all aspects of life in the U.S. Founded in 1972 in Washington, D.C, the organization now has 11 chapters throughout the U.S. and Puerto Rico. Centro holds the New York City chapter records that contain reports, minutes, press releases and some photographs.

Topics: Organizations and Leaders, Women; Social Reform

📅 1980s - 2002	📦 7	🔴 18	🔍 Inventory

The collection consists of interviews conducted by Michael Lapp with several migration division officers, including Luis Cardona, Joseph Monserrat, director of the division from 1951 to 1969, and Alan Perl, the lawyer who dealt with the seasonal farm workers' contracts negotiated by the division. This collection complements the OGPRUS Migration Division records.

Topics: Migration and Settlement, Politics

📅 ca. 1988	📦 8 audiocassettes	🔴 1	🔍 Inventory

49

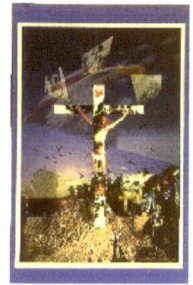

The Laster collection consists of artifacts by the artist, including a piece on the Three Kings, as well as a piece called Vejigante,both made from papier mâché on a wooden base. One is a digital print entitled "The New Millenium," featuring surreal imagery of a man on a cross with a Coca-Cola symbol on it, and the other is a poster entitled "Haciendo Patria,"which features Puerto Rican Nationalist Leader Pedro Albizu Campos.

Topics: Community Welfare; Education; Organizations and Leaders

1998-2001   1.0   1   Description

The Tato Laviera Collection

Tato Laviera (b. 1951) is a Puerto Rican poet who migrated to New York in 1960. Laviera's poetry is written in both Spanish and English, but more often in "Spanglish" and addresses issues such as race and cultural identity affecting Puerto Ricans in the U.S. The collection consists of documents, including biographical information, poems, plays and collaborative projects.

Topics: Literature; Community Welfare; Education; Organizations and Leaders

1960s - present   0.12   5   Inventory

The Lou Lemos The Great Mambo Dancer Script Collection

Playwright. *The Great Mambo Dancer* is a two act play by Lou Lemos copyrighted in 1979.

Topics: Arts and Culture. Literature

1971-2000   0.05   1   Inventory

The Long Island Historical Society Puerto Rican Oral History Transcriptions Collection

The Long Island Historical Society initiated the Puerto Rican Oral History Project in 1973. Over 75 interviews were conducted documenting the experiences of Brooklyn residents who arrived from Puerto Rico between 1917-1940. The original audio interviews are now housed at the Brooklyn Historical Society. Transcriptions are available.

Topics: Migration and Settlement; Community; Organization and Leaders

1917-1940, 1976   1.0   1   Inventory

The Anthony López Papers

Community leader and executive director of ASPIRA of New York, Inc.   López demonstrated commitment to educational opportunity and leadership development for Latino youth. The papers include documentation of his early experiences in leadership positions, organizational records as well as a collection of family photos. The collection consists of letters, clippings, flyers, memoranda, minutes, reports, photographs, proposals, programs, newsletters and notes.

Topics: Community Welfare; Education; Organizations and Leaders

...2001   1.5   3   Finding Aid

The Edwin López Papers

Trade unionist and member of the I.B.E.W. (International Brotherhood of Electrical Workers), where he has served as business representative and national political coordinator, López was also chapter manager and executive secretary of the New York City chapter of National Electrical Contractors Association (NECA). The collection includes correspondence, photographs, newspaper clippings, journals, audiocassettes, videotapes and legal documents.

Topics: Labor and Occupation; Business

1966-2000   2.5   9   Inventory

The José López Papers

Former field representative for the AFL-CIO in New York and member of the 65th Infantry during the Korean War. Collection contains biographical information, documents related to the Hispanic Labor Committee, the Congressional Hispanic Caucus and the Santiago Iglesias Education Society, identification cards, correspondence and photographs. Includes six videos documenting the activities of the Santiago Iglesias Education Society.

Topics: Labor and Occupation; Community Welfare; Organization and Leaders

1950-1994   0.5   5   Inventory

The Lillian López Papers

Library administrator, among the first Puerto Rican librarians in the New York Public Library system (NYPL) and a pioneer in providing services and creating programs for underserved communities. Collection contains information on the programs developed by NYPL to address the needs of its Puerto Rican and Latino constituents, along Evelina Antonetty and Pura Belpré. They are a valuable source of information on the programs developed by NYPL to address the needs of its Puerto Rican and Latino constituents. Notable among the materials are those related to the South Bronx Project and to the puppet theater directed by Pura Belpré. The collection relates to the Pura Belpré Papers in the Centro Archives and highlights how closely the two women worked together. Types of documents included are letters, news clippings, photographs, audio and videocassettes, scrapbooks and play scripts.

Topics: Education

1928-2005   2.67   65   Finding Aid

LP Puerto Rican and Latin America Collection

Artificial Collection consisting of over 650 LP records by Puerto Rican and 400 Latin American musicians donated by Ariel Ruiz, Amilcar Tirado, Anibal Felix, Diana Caballero, William Félix, Pedro Juan Hernández and others.

Topics: Music; Culture

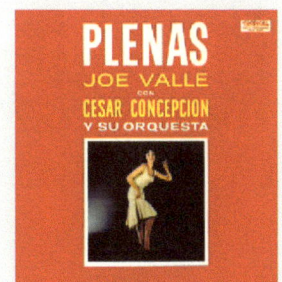

1940-1990s   98.0   15   Inventory

An activist in the movement for school decentralization and member of EQUAL, an organization devoted to improving and integrating the New York City public schools, Lurie has also worked for seven years as director of the Parent Leadership Training Institute at the United Bronx Parents, Inc. (UBP). The collection contains materials that document efforts to integrate and aid the burgeoning Puerto Rican population of East Harlem in the early 1950s. Among these are papers on Americans for Democratic Action, and the East Harlem Project, which focused on schooling issues. Other documents of interest include a proposal from ASPIRA (of New York, Inc.) and files on the People's Board of Education whose members also included Evelina Antonetty, founder of UBP. The papers also contain information on Lurie's work in the Washington Heights section of Manhattan at a time when a significant population of Puerto Ricans still resided there.

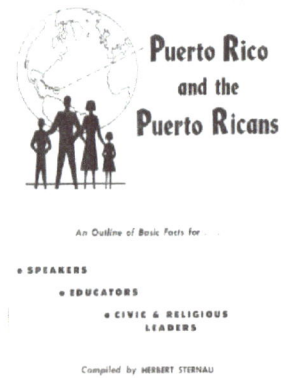

Puerto Rico and the Puerto Ricans

An Outline of Basic Facts for .

- SPEAKERS
  - EDUCATORS
    - CIVIC & RELIGIOUS LEADERS

Compiled by HERBERT STERNAU

Topics: Education; Community

📅 1950s   📦 19.0   ⏱ 14   🔍 Inventory

The Luyanda-Fernández Family Collection

El Saltarín de Ebano

The collection contains photographs, newspaper clippings and books. Among the individuals covered are Juan Luyanda Fernández, a high jumper who competed internationally for Puerto Rico, and his cousin Dalilah Torres Fernádez, who migrated to the U.S. in the1960s. The collection focuses on family activities in New York and Puerto Rico.

Topics: Family and Community Life

📅 1938-2005   📦 2.0   ⏱ 23   🔍 Inventory

The George Malavé Photograph

Photographer who donated a photocomposition of Tito Puente playing timbales.

Topics: Music; Folklore

📅 c1980s   📦 0.01   ⏱ 1   🔍 Inventory

The Adál Maldonado Time Capsule Collection

Artist who forms part of the Nuyorican scene. The collection consists of a time capsule with some artifacts selected by Adál.

Topics: Art; Culture

📅 2010   📦 4.0   ⏱ 14   🔍 Inventory

The collection consists of documents from the papers of Maldonado, Miguelángelo Rodríguez, Pacheco Padró and others. The majority are programs and flyers from various cultural, opera, and theater events and activities, including the 1972 to 1983 Festival Casals in Puerto Rico. A highlight of the collection deals with the discrimination faced by English speakers in Puerto Rico. Also included are a gay short story and literature correspondence.

Topics: Arts; Literature

📅 1954-1987   📦 0.5   🕐 5   🔍 Inventory

Artificial collection grouped by provenance. The Maps Collection consists of 80 items depicting political boundaries in Puerto Rico, geography and demography. The collection also includes maps of the Caribbean archipelago, East Harlem and New York. Highlights of this collection are a 1973 Copperplate engraved map of Puerto Rico, by S. Giovanni, and a copy of a 1576 early map of the island, both in mint condition. Collection includes 80 items.

Topics: Migration and Settlements

📅 1898-1930   📦 80 items   🕐 1   🔍 Inventory

Marcano was one of the foremost Puerto Rican bandleaders, composers, and vocalists of the 1930s and 1940s in New York City. He was founder and director of the Cuarteto Marcano, one of the most popular bands of this time in the bolero style, which consists of soulful ballads dealing with the universal theme of love. Marcano worked closely with performers Pedro Flores, Pedro Ortíz Dávila, Bobby Capó and Tito Rodríguez. The collection consists of documents such as flyers and newspaper clippings, as well as photographs of "Piquito" Marcano and other artists.

Topics: Arts; Music; Performers

📅 1920-1972   📦 0.12   🕐 27   🔍 Inventory

Los Pleneros de la 21 is a non-profit organization serving the Puerto Rican/Latino community and based in El Barrio, East Harlem. Los Pleneros is also a performing ensemble, preserving the Afro-Puerto Rican traditions of the bomba and plena. The Cuba collection consists of 14 photographs and two videos photographs relating to the Puerto Rican musical group's visit to Cuba in 2003, which was co-sponsored by Centro and documented by Hiram Maristany.

Topics: Music; Folklore

📅 2003   📦 0.5   🕐 14.0   🔍 Inventory

53

Photographer and former Merchant Marine. This collection is an important resource for its impressive visuals, which document the life and activities of individuals, families and organizations that make up the Puerto Rican experience in New York City, as well as the experience of other Hispanic groups as seen through the lens of photographer Martí. They primarily capture the time period between the 1940s and 1980s and the major social and political events, leaders and movements of those times. The entire collection is a visual testament of the Latino/Puerto Rican presence in New York City. The collection contains 98 cubic feet of prints and 78 cubic feet of negatives.

Topics: Family and Community Life; Migration and Settlement; General

| | 1920s-1990 | | 166.0 | | 403 | | Finding Aid |

The Susana Martínez Collection

Puerto Rican poet and an active member of the Puerto Rican community in El Barrio. The collection consists of four published poetry books and anthologies, two unpublished manuscripts, notebooks and writings, original paintings, award certificates from various organizations, newspaper clippings, event programs, newsletters, correspondence and copyright documents for her writings.

Topics: Arts; Literature; Culture

| | 1964 - 1996 | | 1.2 | | 6 | | Inventory |

Dough McGee Photographs of Jorge Soto

Contains 3 of McGee's photos of artist Jorge Soto.

Topics: Arts

| | | | 0.01 | | 1 | | Inventory |

The José Rafael Méndez Steamships Collection

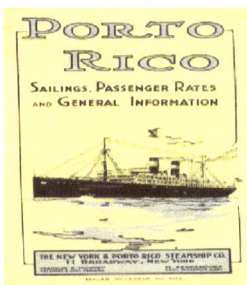

This microfilm collection contains a display of steamship artifacts, manifests, and programs by the Porto Rico Line Steamship. Artifacts and documents in this display were recovered from steamships en-route to New York and/or other Caribbean destinations. The images and mementos of tourists, crewmembers and migrants will help recreate their journeys and their rich and multifaceted stories.

Topics: Migration and Settlement

| | 1906-1940 | | 0.05 | | 19 | | Inventory |

WE TOOK THE STREETS

FIGHTING FOR LATINO RIGHTS
WITH
THE YOUNG LORDS

MIGUEL "Mickey" MELENDEZ
Foreword by Jose Torres

ST. MARTIN'S PRESS NEW YORK

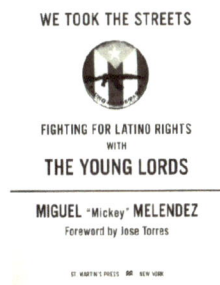

Melendez is an activist for Latino and Puerto Rican rights. He has held senior positions in the New York City government and has taught in the black and Hispanic studies department at Baruch College. He is also the recipient of the Charles Revson Fellowship (2004-05) at Columbia University. The collection is made up exclusively of edited galleys of Meléndez's manuscript *We Took the Streets* (2003).

Topics: Organizations and Leaders, Social Reform; Politics, Government; and Law

📅 2003   📦 0.25   🧭 2   🔍 Inventory

First Puerto Rican woman elected to a state legislature in the U.S. mainland. Méndez was born in Puerto Rico and married into a respected East Harlem political family. Her father-in-law, Tony Méndez, was the first Puerto Rican district leader in Manhattan. She became an active leader in the area of voter registration drives throughout the nation. Méndez served as senator to the New York State legislature from 1984 to 2004, becoming the first Puerto Rican woman to serve in that position. The collection is made up of correspondence, photographs and organizational files.

Topics: Family and Community; Organizations and Leaders; Politics, Government, and Law

📅 1950s-2004   📦 66.0   🧭 15   🔍 Inventory

Public servant at the state, city and federal level, serving in organizations such as the Equal Economic Employment Opportunity Commission. He was director of the New York City Commission on Human Rights and the New York State Division of Human Rights. The collection documents the participation of Mercado and other Latinos in Republican Party politics, information made all the more interesting because Latinos have traditionally favored the Democratic Party. It also deals with the Puerto Rican status issue, particularly the links between the statehood movement and the Partido Nuevo Progresista on the island and with Puerto Ricans in the United States. The papers consist of reports, correspondence, writings, news clippings and photographs.

Topics: Organizations and Leaders; Politics, Government, and Law; Social Reform

📅 1960s-1999   📦 10.47   🧭 21   🔍 Finding Aid

Arranger, guitarist and musical director for the salsa band Saoco. Collection consists of videotapes, audiocassettes, CDs and flyers and other promotional documents for Saoco, and documents on Puerto Rican poets, writers, theater, playwrights and Taíno culture.

Topics: Music; Arts; Community Life

WILLIAM MILLAN
Y SU
SAOCO

📅 1970-1997   📦 0.25   🧭 5   🔍 Inventory

55

The collection consists of correspondence, reports, clippings and bulletins belonging to Miller, who served as the Commissioner of Education in Puerto Rico from 1915-1930. He also wrote Historia de Puerto Rico. The collection documents the transition of the educational medium from English only, which had been established in 1898, after the American occupation, to Spanish in the lower grades and English in the higher grades. This collection was deaccessioned from the Forrest R. Polk Archives.

Topics: Education

| 📅 1915-1930 | 📦 0.12 | 🕐 6 | 🔍 Inventory |

The Graciany Miranda Archilla Papers

Poet, journalist and essayist, and a co-founder of the literary movement Atalayismo. The collection also provides useful insights into the political and cultural milieu of Puerto Rico in the 1930s and 1940s and of the Puerto Rican community in New York of the 1950s and 1960s. It consists of correspondence, published and unpublished poetry, essays, critical reviews, clippings and photographs.

Topics: Arts and Literature

| 📅 1911-1991 | 📦 6.3 | 🕐 13 | 🔍 Finding Aids |

The Marlis Momber Lower East Side Photograph Collection

German born photographer who has documented the Lower East Side for over 30 years. Collection consists of contact sheets, prints, a DVD version of the film *Viva Loisaida*, postcards for exhibitions, clippings, biographical information, press releases, flyers, books featuring Momber's work, a painting with an image modeled on one of Momber's images and copies of *Loisaida: The Lower East Side Magazine*.

Topics: Arts; Community

| 📅 1970s-2009 | 📦 3.5 | 🕐 138 | 🔍 Inventory |

The Joseph Monserrat Papers

A government official and community leader, the Papers document Monserrat's role in the formation and implementation of the policies of the government of Puerto Rico regarding the migration of Puerto Ricans to the U.S. The materials cover the areas of community development, bilingual education, school decentralization, civil rights, electoral politics, police brutality and corruption, community organizations, farm labor, inter-group relations and the internal workings of the Migration Division and the Board of Education of the City of NY. Among the personalities represented in the collection are Luis Muñoz Marín, Herman Badillo, Rafael Hernández Colón, Robert García, Leonard Covello and Nydia Velázquez. The records consist primarily of personal documents, correspondence, writings, appointment books, directories, reports, news clippings, programs and photographs.

Topics: Organizations and Leaders; Politics, Government and Law; Social Refor, Labor and Occupation

| 📅 1953-2005 | 📦 12.56 | 🕐 24 | 🔍 Finding Aids |

The Jose F. Morales Toxic Avengers Records

The Toxic Avengers is a student group founded at El Puente Community Center in Williamsburg, Brooklyn, in 1987. Concerned itself with issues of pollution and environmental safety in the immediate community. Collection includes memoranda, agendas, correspondence, photographs, publications, clippings, reports, a banner and a reel of 8-mm film.

Topics: Health and Community Welfare

| 1990-1991 | 2.0 | 93 | Inventory |

Muévete Records

A youth conference and organization founded by the National Latinas Caucus and affiliated with the Puerto Rican Association for Community Affairs. It addresses leadership issues and involvement in cultural and community affairs. The collection comprises of conference proceedings, programs, posters, announcements and other promotional materials.

Topics: Leaders and Organizations; Culture; Welfare and Community Life; Social Reform; Youth

| 1992-1999 | 5.0 | 6 | Inventory |

The Mujica Family Collection

The Mujica Family Documents are a genealogical collection consisting of .05 cubic feet of items, including four family photographs taken in Brooklyn, New York, and personal documents including two original war ration books and a postcard, dating from 1933 to 1952. This collection was donated by Diana Youngfleisch. Inventory available

Topics: Family and Community Life; Migration and Settlement

| 1933-1952 | 0.05 | 6 | Inventory |

57

N-P

The National Congress of Puerto Rican Rights Collection

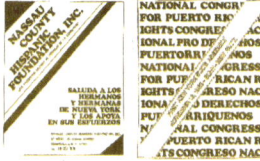

Civil rights organization aiming to unite different groups and sectors of the Puerto Rican community such as professionals, laborers, students, artists and others in efforts to combat discrimination and inequality. There is information about the events, including publicity, memoranda, bulletins, photographs and programs of various events and chapters of the organization.

Topics: Leaders and organizations, Community Life

📅 1981-1991   📦 0.50   🧭 1   🔍 Description

National Latinas Caucus Records

The principal goal of the organization is to empower women in local communities by organizing and developing networks around issues of common concern, to provide opportunities for personal and professional advancement and to foster a stronger sense of self-awareness. Special projects include El Barrio Renaissance, an effort to create low- and moderate-income residential units by renovating city-owned vacant buildings, and Economic/Leadership Development mini-courses for Latinas.

Topics: Leaders and Organizations; Health and Community Welfare; Women

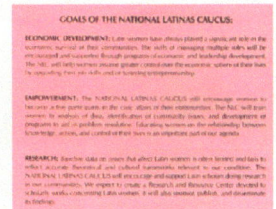

📅 1985-1991   📦 1.0   🧭 5   🔍 Description

National Puerto Rican Forum (NPRF) Records

Founded in 1957 by Antonia Pantoja, the National Puerto Rican Forum provides education, training, advocacy and information to prepare individuals for meaningful employment. NPRF is the oldest national Puerto Rican organization in the United States.

Topics: Education; Labor and Education; Community Welfare

📅 1970s   📦 6.90   🧭 5   🔍 Inventory

The Sonia Nieto Papers

A professor of language, literacy and culture, Nieto is an expert in the fields of multicultural and bilingual education and Puerto Rican children's literature. She is the author of numerous books and is involved in organizations that focus on educational equity and social justice. Her papers contain photographs, oral history interviews, writings and other materials.

Topics: Education; Culture; Social Reform

📅 1970s-2004   📦 30.40   🧭 1   🔍 Inventory

Noriega worked as special assistant for migrant labor for the State of New York Department Labor (1977 to 1983) and was a member of the Governor's Advisory Committee for Hispanic Affairs (1984 to 1994). Noriega formed a production company, Noriega Productions. As part of a documentary project, he researched and interviewed influential Puerto Rican figures. The collection consists of documents such as biographical information clippings, correspondence, bulletins and reports, and photographs of political officials.

Topics: Labor and Occupation; Organization and Leaders

Proud moment

📅 1937-1994	📦 0.25	🔴 7	🔍 Inventory

The Louis Nuñez Papers

Civil rights activist, former executive director of ASPIRA of New York, Inc. and ASPIRA of America, former president of the National Puerto Rican Coalition and former staff director for the U.S. Commission on Civil Rights. The collection consists of personal and professional correspondence, annual reports and newsletters from the NPRC and remarks from his period as staff director for the U.S. Commission on Civil Rights. In addition, there are photographs that document Nuñez's many professional roles.

Topics: Organizations and Leaders; Social Reform

📅 1963-2006	📦 4.1	🔴 5	🔍 Inventory

The Records of the Offices of the Government of Puerto Rico in the United States (OGPRUS)

The Records of the Offices of the Government of Puerto Rico in the United States (OGPRUS) consist of records generated by a central office and various regional and local offices operated by the Government of Puerto Rico in the continental United States (1930-1993). The collection includes records for: **Bureau of Identification and Documentation (1930-1948)**; the **Office of Information for Puerto Rico (1945-1949)**; the **Migration Division (1948 -1989)**; and the **Department of Community Affairs in the United States, (1989 -1993)** a cabinet-level department, which superceded the Migration Division.

Topics: Migration; Labor and Ocuupation; Community and Family Life.

📅 1930s-1993	📦 1860.0	🔴 47	🔍 Finding Aids

60

The collection includes the Ruth M. Reynolds, Centro de Estudios Puertorriqueños, and West Coast Puerto Rican Elders Oral History projects. It is comprised of audio cassettes and oral history transcripts that stand as an invaluable resource of alternative documentation for many of the personal papers and collections within the Archives. Far reaching in their scope, the audio cassettes document lectures, seminars, colloquia, and research conducted by journalists, political figures and artists. They include recordings on political education sessions, original interviews with participants in the Language Policy Task Force's project on *Bilingualism and Bilingual Education in the Puerto Rican Community*, as well as numerous oral histories included in the seminal project *Puerto Ricans in NY: Voices of the Migration*, along with those of other noted political and cultural figures.

Topics: Migration; Labor and Occupation; Community and Family Life.

📅 1960s-1990	📦 12.0	💿 5	🔍 Inventory

Records of the O.P. Art (Organization of Puerto Rican Artists)

O.P. Art is a not-for-profit founded in 1993 by a group of New York-based Puerto Rican artists to preserve and promote their artwork and cultural identity. The collection highlights the vibrancy and cultural relevance of Puerto Rican artists of the diaspora and helps to expose their largely underrecognized talent and contributions. O.P. Art members are part of a grassroots artist collective, which consists of emerging, established and well-known Puerto Rican artists. Many established institutions, including the Smithsonian, the Museum of Modern Art and the *New York Times* have recognized the work of these artists.

Members have taken their artwork outside of traditional venues such as museums and galleries and into the community. They have provided an outlet for the public to encounter, interact and explore creative works and Puerto Rican culture while examining larger social issues.

The records includes correspondence, bylaws, press releases, news clippings, promotional materials, photographs and artist biographies. The collection illustrates the tireless work and administrative maneuvering required for creating and managing this type of endeavor.

Topics: Arts, Culture; Artists; Organizations

📅 1993-2012	📦 2.0	💿 36	🔍 Inventory

The Awilda Orta Collection

Bilingual education director from 1980 to 1983 under Chancellor Anthony Alvarado. She worked previously in District 4 in East Harlem. She was an active member and officer of the Puerto Rican Educators Association, the National Association for Bilingual Education and the New York State Association for Bilingual Education.

Topics: Education; Community

📅 1964-1997	📦 5.0	💿 9	🔍 Description

61

Photographer, documentary filmmaker and co-founder of the Nubia Music Society, the collection documents the creator's two main interests: Latin music and the South Bronx. It is a resource for research on the history of the South Bronx, and, in particular, the Puerto Rican community in the Longwood neighborhood, from the dire 1970s to its rebirth in the 1990s. The collection also serves to understand the New York Latin jazz and salsa scene and its legendary stars in a musical and historical context: Ray Barretto, Celia Cruz, Frank "Machito" Grillo, Charlie Palmieri and Tito Puente. It contains materials on the political movements, demonstrations and protests in the city. Community institutions such as the Puerto Rican Day Parade, the Puerto Rican Traveling Theatre and the United Bronx Parents are also represented. It includes the Society's papers, correspondence, newspaper clippings, articles, pamphlets, photographs (negatives, prints and slides), and audiovisual materials.

Topics: Arts; Culture; Music; Artists

📅	1940s-2006	📦	42.0	⏱	13	🔍	Finding Aid

Antonio Pacheco Padró was a political journalist who founded a Puerto Rican Revolutionary Party in New York in 1934 and served as a volunteer in the Spanish Civil War in 1937. The collection consists of Padró's certificate of incorporation into Editorial La Prensa.

Topics: Politics; Government, and Law; Social Reform; Journalism

📅	1963	📦	2.0	⏱	5	🔍	Inventory

The Muriel Pagán Collection

Former director of Bilingual Education for the Division of Special Education within the New York City Board of Education, Assistant Principal from 1968 to 1979 at PS 25 in the Southeast Bronx, the first totally bilingual school in the Northeast region of New York State. Collection includes correspondence, information on PS 25 – The Bilingual School; the Office of Bilingual Services; education programs to conferences on bilingual education; the proceedings of a conference held by the Department of Education of the Commonwealth of Puerto Rico; clippings; flyers; and some publications.

Topics: Education

📅	1960-1980	📦	0.50	⏱	6	🔍	Inventory

Vicente "Panama" Alba Pérez, activist and community organizer. Collection consists of the manuscript for book titled PanaRican. Vicente Panama together with Richie Pérez, Mickey Melendez and others, acting under the auspices of the Committee for the Freedom of the Puerto Rican Nationalist, organized a takeover of the Statue of Liberty on October 1977.

Topics: Leaders and Organizations; Family and Community Life; Education; Family and Community Life; Social Reform; Politics

📅	2008	📦	0.2	⏱	1	🔍	Description

The Antonia Pantoja Papers

The papers help document the vibrant and multifaceted life of one of the great institutional pioneers of the Puerto Rican community. In addition, they lend insight into the nature and origins of the organizations founded by Pantoja and the extent to which they chronicle her personal and intellectual growth. This rich collection, includes personal affects from her early years in Puerto Rico, historical materials on the inception and initial growth of ASPIRA of New York, Inc., as well as a vast array of photographs documenting all phases of her life. The collection also documents the evolution of Pantoja's consciousness as a black Puerto Rican woman and a Nuyorican, and the subsequent contributions of these identities to her professional development. The materials consist of correspondence, memoranda, photographs, flyers, clippings, proposals, reports, speeches, writings, awards, posters and videotapes.

Topics: Leaders and Organizations; Education; Health and Community Welfare; Family and Community Life; Education; Family and Community Life; Social Reform; Politics , Government, and Law;

1923-2002	24.0	47	Finding Aids

The Pepatian Records

A South Bronx-based organization dedicated to creating, presenting and supporting contemporary multidisciplinary work from Latino and Bronx-based artists who speak to and from the Afro-Caribbean-Latino identity of the South Bronx. Founded by Pepón Osorio (visual artist, MacArthur Fellow), Merián Soto (Bessie-award winning choreographer) and Patricia Bradshaw (choreographer/dancer) as an artists' collective in 1983. The collection includes a binder with information on Merián Soto's choreographic career and 10 videocassettes featuring her choreographic work.

Topics: Arts; Culture

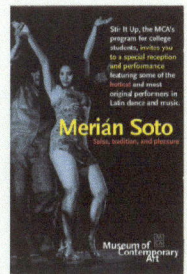

1980s	0.50	105	Description

The Federico Pérez Collection

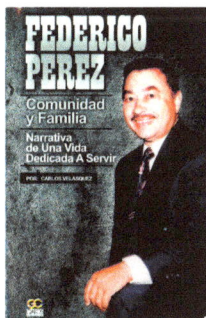

This collection is made up of one folder of photographs that document, among other things, the Puerto Rican Day Parade, the Puerto Rican Community Development Project, local clubs and associations, as well as several community events.

Topics: Community Life

1950-1980	0.1	5	Description

The Nélida Pérez Collection

Former Centro's librarian and archivist, the collection contains several art works by artist Jorge Soto, sound recordings and some family photographs

Topics: Arts and Culture, Migration and Settlement

1950's-1980s	0.25	1	Description

The papers chronicle the political trajectory and organizing efforts of one of the Puerto Rican communities' most dedicated advocates and activists. Moreover, they help document grassroots efforts at combating police brutality and racially motivated violence and aiding community struggles for the betterment of social and economic conditions for Puerto Ricans, Latinos and other people of color in New York City. The collection includes materials on the National Congress for Puerto Rican Rights and the Justice Committee, numerous files on local community organizations and initiatives, as well as a solid collection of leftist and Latino-focused newspapers. In addition, contained is a large selection of audio visuals and photographs, which help capture the vibrancy of the political and social movements. They consist of personal documents, clippings, articles, photographs, speeches, certificates, flyers, correspondence, audiocassettes, videocassettes, slides, CDs, DVDs and artifacts.

Topics: Education; Health and Community Welfare; Politics, Government, and Law, Organizations and Leaders; Social Reform

1918-2006   22.0   1   Finding Aid

The Sofía Pérez Photographs Collection

Community activist and organizer in Brooklyn., she was active in the Association of Puerto Rican Women, Fiesta Folklórica and the Puerto Rico Community Development Project (PRCDP). In August 1957, she incorporated and started McKibb Star Social and Athletic Club Inc. Mckibb Star would become the venue for her community activism, political organizing and cultural events. The collection documents her political activism, and the social and cultural events she organized with her community.

Topics: Family Life, Organizations and Leaders, Migration and Settlements

1950-1960s   0.10   1   Description

The Guillermo Pérez-Mesa Puerto Rican Stamps Collection In Memory of José Colón Leucene

Collection of Puerto Rican stamps dating from 1873 to 1971. Most of the stamps are included in the Album de Sellos de Puerto Rico. Among the collection highlights are: early stamps from 1870s to 1898, first stamps in circulation during the early years of United States domination, the 400th anniversary of Puerto Rico's discovery, the First Gubernatorial Election 1949 and the 450th Anniversary (1521-1971) of San Juan City foundation.

Topics: History

1873-1971   0.10   47   Description

The Pedro Pietri Papers

Writer and one of the founders of the Nuyorican poetry movement. The papers help chronicle the creative, productive and, at times, anarchic life of one of the most original and innovative contemporary writers of the Puerto Rican community. In addition, they lend insight of Pietri's literary interests and endeavors, his collaborative relationships with other writers and his editorial process. The papers include extensive original writings, annotated drafts of already published works and original artwork. The collection boasts a large array of handmade artifacts and an impressive assortment of posters and publications documenting artistic activity in New York over the last three decades. The materials consist of correspondence, memoranda, photographs, flyers, clippings, poetry, plays, essays, scripts, awards, posters, programs, videotapes, audiocassettes, artwork and artifacts.

Topics: Arts; Literature; Social Reform

1939-2004   55.0   546   Finding Aid

Corporation created by Robi Draco Rosa, dedicated to the multimedia industry. Collection contains CDs and videos in VHS and Beta format.

Topics: Music; Culture

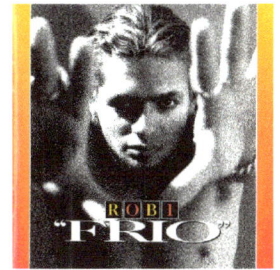

📅 1998-2004   📦 0.50   ⌀ 1   🔍 Description

The Politics Con Sabor Collection

The collection contains materials gathered from a two part documentary produced by Terramax, Inc. and Centro. The film features the Puerto Rican community's involvement and impact on NY State political history. The materials consist of all audio/video interviews, photographs and other original documents, from Judge Irma Vidal Santaella, Reverend Bernardo López, Luis Rodriguez and the family of Adriano Rivera.

Topics: Politic; Organization and Leaders

📅 2006   📦 2.5   ⌀ 1   🔍 Inventory

Postcards Collection

Almost half of the items are souvenir postcards of Puerto Rico, dating from 1898 to the 1970s. These are arranged by town and economic activities, such as sugarcane, coffee, and tobacco. About two-fifths of the postcards are of more recent (1990 to 2006) sociocultural activities in New York, including theatre, music, dance, film and gay and lesbian events. The remaining items are postcards of the Antilles; Cuba, the Dominican Republic and Haiti.

Topics: Culture, Organizations and Leaders, Music

📅 1898-2010s   📦 2.0   ⌀ 1   🔍 Inventory

The Prayer Books Collection

Collection consists of 40 small, pocket-sized prayer books/booklets in the Catholic tradition of Puerto Rico. The prayers are to saints, such as San Gabriel, Santa Isabel and San José. Also included is a blank Catholic identification card, which expresses the holder's wishes to have the sacraments administered in the case of an accident.

Topics: Religion; Culture

📅 1940-1950s   📦 0.30   ⌀ 1   🔍 Inventory

Collection composed of 9 reels of Hispanic journals and periodicals gathered from various collections in the Archives in order to group them by title of publication. Included: *Alba de Nueva York, Boletín de la Liga Puertorriqueña, Cascabeles, Mundo Latino, Puerto Rico y Nueva York, Vida Hispana, La Voz de Puerto Rico, El Boricua, En Marcha,* and many others.

Topics: Culture, Organizations and Leaders, Music

📅 1923-1969   📦 6.0   💿 1   🔍 Inventory

The Pregones Red Rose Collection

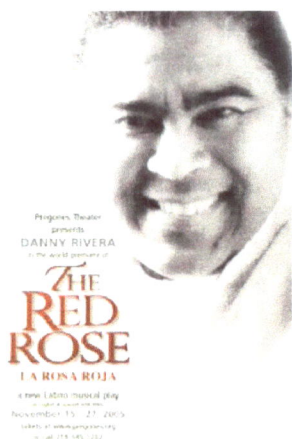

The Pregones Theater is a Bronx-based ensemble performing original plays and musical theater rooted in Puerto Rican/Latin culture. Since 1979, the theater has produced more than 50 new plays and presented twice as many visiting performing artists. In 2005, the theater produced a play based on the life of Jesus Colón called *The Red Rose* starring Danny Rivera. Colón was a writer dedicated to chronicling the Puerto Rican migrant experience and is today considered an iconic figure in Puerto Rican diaspora history. The Pregones Red Rose Collection consists of playbills from the November-December 2005 season, an invitation to the opening night gala event for *The Red Rose*, and other mailings announcing the play.

Topics: Arts; Culture, Organizations and Leaders, Music

📅 2005   📦 0.12   💿 1   🔍 Inventory

The Puerto Rican Communities Collection

The Puerto Rican Communities Collection consists of documents, reports, conference materials and photographs on Puerto Rican communities in the U.S., including California, Illinois (Chicago), Florida and Hawaii. Puerto Ricans in: California contains 71 photographs and digital images from the Western Region Puerto Rican Council, El Dia de San Juan Festival in San José; Chicago conference materials from the fifth conference of the Puerto Rican Studies Association, held in 2002, as well as several flyers on community organizations and events; Florida contains informational brochures for Centro de Cultura Puertorriqueña de la Florida and Asociación Borinqueña de Florida Central; Hawaii contains a collection of poems by Camacho Souza and Austin Dias, a course catalog for the summer 2000 session at University of Hawai'i at Manoa Outreach College, and a year 2000 calendar celebrating 100 years of Puerto Ricans on Maui. Also in the collection is a program for the Puerto Rican Community Conference, held April 19-20, 1969 at Baruch College, CUNY.

Topics: Community Life; Migration and Settlement

📅 1990-2002   📦 0.12   💿 1   🔍 Inventory

Puerto Rican Community Development Project, Puerto Rican Day Parade Collection

This collection is made up of one folder of photographs that document the Puerto Rican Day Parade, the Puerto Rican Community Development Project, local clubs and associations, as well as several community events.

Topics: Community Life

📅 1950-1980   📦 0.1   🧭 5   🔍 Description

The San Juan & San Germán Delegations to the Nations Parade Collection

The collection consists of six photographs of the Puerto Rican Delegations in a Nation's Parade.

Topics: Community Life; Religion; Culture

📅 1940s   📦 0.1   🧭 5   🔍 Inventory

Puerto Rican Family Institute, Inc., Records

The institute is a multiprogram, family-oriented health and human service agency whose primary mission is to prevent family disintegration and enhance the self-sufficiency of the Latino community. Programs operate in the continental United States and in Puerto Rico. Collection is made up of a report detailing the official proceedings of the First Forum on the Human Rights of the Puerto Rican Migrant Family from 1983.

Topics: Community Life; Social Reform

📅 1960s   📦 0.12   🧭 5   🔍 Description

Puerto Rican Legal Defense and Education Fund (PRLDEF) Records

The PRLDEF is the major civil rights advocacy organization for the Puerto Rican community of the US. Headquartered in New York and taking its place among institutions such as the National Association for the Advancement of Colored People Legal Defense Fund (NAACP-LDF) and the Mexican American Legal Defense and Educational Fund (MALDEF). The organizational records are a significant contribution to the study of the history of Puerto Ricans in the U.S. While they are obviously a rich resource for legal scholars, the research potential of the records encompasses numerous areas. They will be of value to historical and humanistic scholarship in the field of ethnic studies, education and political rights, among others. This collection makes a major contribution in an area of American social and political history that has been sparsely documented. The holdings consist of administrative records, minutes, correspondence, executive directors files, and presidential and general counsel, subject files and all closed litigation files from 1972 to 1988.

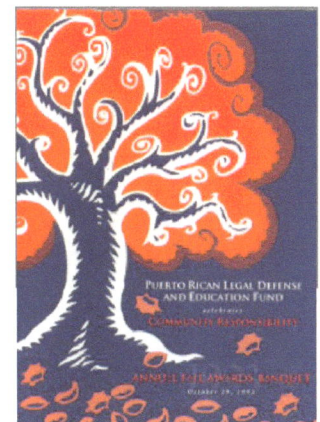

Topics: Education; Politic, Government, and Law; Labor and Ocuupation; Social Reform

📅 1973-1993   📦 232.0   🧭 8   🔍 Finding Aid

67

Puerto Rican Migration Research Consortium

The collection is made up of correspondence, membership forms and financial information about the consortium.

Topics: Migration and Settlement

1960s - present

📅 1977-1983   📦 0.5   🧭 1   🔍 Description

Puerto Rican Studies Association Chicago Conference Collection

Puerto Ricans in Chicago contains conference materials from the 5th conference of the Puerto Rican Studies Association, held October 3-5, 2002, as well as several flyers on community organizations and events.

Topics: Organizations and culture, Education

📅 2002   📦 .10   🧭 1   🔍 Description

Puerto Ricans in California: Medina Echevarría Family Collection

Puerto Ricans in California contains 71 photographs and digital images from the Medina Echevarria Family Western Region Puerto Rican Council, and El Día de San Juan Festival in San José in June of 1999.

Topics: Community Life; Migration and Settlement

📅 1990s   📦 .10   🧭 5   🔍 Inventory

Puerto Ricans in Virgin Island Collection

Collection contains event programs, postcards, newspapers, newsletters, a t-shirt and a small poster documenting the Puerto Rican presence in the United States Virgin Islands. In particular, the materials chronicle the activities of the Virgin Islands-Puerto Rico Friendship Committee.

Topics: Migration and Settlement; Community Life

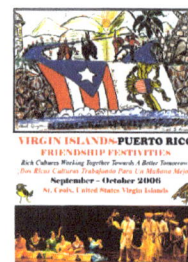

📅 2004-2006   📦 0.25   🧭 5   🔍 Description

Q-R

The Quality of Life in/Calidad de vida en Loisaida, Inc. is a free community magazine relating topics and issues impacting the Lower East Side aka Loisaida residents. Most of the articles, photographs and artwork are by the community residents.

Topics: Migration and Settlement; Culture, Organizations and Leaders

1978-1991   1.0   1   Description

The Diana Ramírez de Arellano Papers

Author of poetry and literary criticism, the collection documents cultural expression among Puerto Ricans in NY City, particularly in the period of the 1960s and 1970s. In addition to documenting numerous artistic and literary activities, the papers provide a detailed look at the work and history of the Ateneo Puertorriqueño de Nueva York and an important contemporary writer's artistic and literary activities. The materials consist of letters, minutes, articles, books, programs, newspaper clippings, audiotapes and phonograph records.

Topics: Arts and Culture; Education; Literature; Organizations and Leaders; Gender and Sexuality

1947-1997   3.81   13   Finding Aid

The Tina Ramírez Collection

Dancer and choreogapher of Mexican and Puerto Rican descent. Ramírez founded Ballet Hispánico dance company in 1970 and served for 39 years as its artistic director. She was awarded the National Medal of Arts in 2005. The materials include news clippings, notebooks, photos, slides, documents and videos. The contents of the collection were used by the school for advertisement purposes. The collection also contains oversize photographs, videos in several formats and several audio recordings in different formats

Topics: Arts and Culture; Education; Dance

1970-2010   3.50   1   Inventory

Realidades Humberto Cintrón Collection

The first national Latino public affairs bilingual television series for adults ever funded by the Corporation for Public Broadcast produced at WNET, Channel 13, NY City (1971 to 1977). Topics include the Young Lords, ASPIRA and migrant women. This collection consists of papers, reports, banner, photographs, negatives and 3/4 inch video masters. Humberto Cintrón is best known for his role as host, writer and executive producer of *Realidades*.

Topics: Culture; Education; Organization and Leaders;

1971-1979   3.0   1   Description

The Papers inform researchers about the contributions that Puerto Ricans, particularly these three individuals, made to the establishment and expansion of drug abuse treatment and prevention services in New York City as well as throughout New York State and beyond. This collection traces their leadership in the drug treatment field from the early 1970s until, as in the case of Carlos Pagán, the present. Although small, the collection documents the personal lives and professional accomplishments of the rehabilitation program pioneers through biographical profiles, personal writings, newspaper clippings and organizational documents. Other highlights of the collection include records from the New York State Division of Substance Abuse and the accompanying materials from the Committee on Government Integrity, which lend insight into the growth of substance abuse programs and services in New York, the role of Puerto Rican leaders in this process and the government investigations into allegations of funding improprieties. Also of note is a Storycorp recording by Pagán, which traces the development of drug rehabilitation programs and services in NY City and the numerous Puerto Ricans who were a part of these efforts. Included are awards, correspondence, clippings, flyers, notes, programs, publications, photographs, writings and a CD and DVD.

Topics: Health and Community Welfare; Gender and Sexuality; Organizations and Leaders; Social Reform

| 📅 1967-2008 | 📦 1.5 | 💿 1 | 🔍 Finding Aid |

The Clara Restrepo and Archilla Family Papers

The collection consists of 5 portraits belonging to Restrepo and biographical and historical documents from the Archilla Family Reunion, which took place in 1979 in Dallas. Included among the biographical sketches is a piece by Graciany Miranda Archilla, a poet, journalist, essayist and co-founder of an important literary movement, whose papers we hold in our archives.

Topics: Family and Comminity Life

| 📅 1931-1979 | 📦 0.05 | 💿 5 | 🔍 Inventory |

The Luis O. Reyes Papers

Educator, scholar, activist, and university professor. The papers are a valuable resource for the study and understanding of public education and the Puerto Rican/ Latino community in NY City from the 1980s-1990s. The documents in this collection fill a significant information gap on important organizations such as ASPIRA of New York, Inc., the Puerto Rican/Latino Educational Roundtable and the Latino Commission on AIDS. Among the papers are: bilingual and multicultural education, minority students, the rights of non-English speakers in the U.S., minority language rights, HIV/AIDS, school dropouts, educational reform, Latino representation on the Board of Education, public school demographics and numerous local and national education associations. The bulk of the materials consist of administrative files. There are letters, memoranda, notes, notebooks, minutes, reports, announcements and newspaper clippings.

Topics: Education; Organizations and Leaders; Politics, Government, and Law; Social Reform

| 📅 1961-1998 | 📦 30.12 | 💿 52 | 🔍 Finding Aid |

The papers support research in important areas of Puerto Rican history, as well as in US participation in international human rights. While they are exceedingly rich in insight and information about the development of the Nationalist Party of Puerto Rico and its leader, Albizu Campos, they also contain materials on other independence movements in Puerto Rico, on repression and political prisoners, and on the colonial relationship of the US to Puerto Rico. There is also a good amount of information on the history of the University of Puerto Rico and on student movements. The collection consists of awards, correspondence, writings, subject files, clippings, flyers, notes, programs, publications, photographs, "secret files" known as carpetas and audio cassettes.

Topics: Arts; Literature; Culture; Organization and Leaders; Social Reform; Gender and Sexuality

| 📅 1915-1989 | 📦 21.25 | ⏱ 46 | 🔍 Finding Aid |

The Dennis Rivera Collection

Labor leader and former president of New York's largest health care union, 1199/S.E.I.U. United Healthcare Workers East, currently chairman of the million-member health-care division of the Service Employees International Union. The collection include Rivera's writings, photographs and negatives documenting his personal and professional lives, artifacts and bound volumes of 1199 News.

Topics: Labor and Occupation; Social Reform

| 📅 1987-1996 | 📦 5.25 | ⏱ 1 | 🔍 Inventory |

The Peter Rivera Collection

NY State Assemblyman (1992-2012) representing District 76, which comprises the West Farms, Van Nest, Castle Hill and Parkchester neighborhoods in the Bronx. The materials consist of photographs, press releases, clippings, reports, awards and posters.

Topics: Politics; Government, and Law

| 📅 1992-2012 | 📦 17.0 | ⏱ 10 | 🔍 Inventory |

The Raquel Z. Rivera Hip Hop/Reggaeton Collection

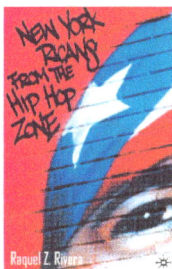

Raquel Z. Rivera is an author and singer-songwriter. She has a Ph.D. in sociology and her areas of scholarly interest include popular music and culture, race and ethnicity, nation and diaspora, and the intersections between Latino and Africana studies. From 2006-2009 she was a researcher at the Center for Puerto Rican Studies, Hunter College, CUNY.The Raquel Z. Rivera Hip Hop/Reggaeton Collection helps document Puerto Rican contributions to the creation and development of hip hop and reggaeton both in the United States and Puerto Rico.

Topics: Music; Culture, Education

Cont. ▶▶

◀◀ Cont.

A rich collection, highlights include an extensive audiocassette and compact disc holdings that feature rare and early recordings by "underground" and Puerto Rico-based "reggae" artists whose work was a precursor to present day reggaeton. The recordings are inclusive of Puerto Rican/Latino rap recordings also from the island and the U.S., as well as several insightful interviews with many of these artists. In addition, the collection also contains essays written by Rivera on hip hop and reggaeton, paper documentation on artists featured on the recordings, videocassettes and DVD's of musical performances and magazines and other publications that capture the cultural and musical impact of hip hop and reggaeton on contemporary Puerto Rican and American societies.

The materials in this collection span the years from 1977 to 2005, with the bulk concentrating on the years 1995 to 2003. They consist of correspondence, photographs, flyers, clippings, writings, publications, videocassettes, DVD's, audiocassettes and compact discs. The materials are in both Spanish and English.

| 📅 1977-2008 | 📦 10.0 | 💿 2 | 🔍 Finding Aid |

The Gloria Rodriguez Calero Collection

Visual artist. Rodríguez Calero was born in Puerto Rico and raised in New York, and for 20 years worked and resided in New Jersey. Her career and services are active in El Barrio and the Lower East Side Communities. Collection measures 4.5 cubic feet and includes correspondence from Lorenzo Homar, a fellow artist, and a number of books, exhibition catalogues and other ephemera. Included as well are sample artworks, posters documenting performances conducted by Augusto Rodríguez and a map of Puerto Rico. The materials date from 1949 to 2006.

Topics: Visual Arts

| 📅 1949-2006 | 📦 4.5 | 💿 5 | 🔍 Inventory |

The Augusto Rodríguez Collection

Rodríguez (1904-1993) was a musician, composer and chorus director. He founded the Choir of the University of Puerto Rico. In 1961, Rodríguez was the recipient of both the Puerto Rican Institute of Culture's and the Puerto Rican Athenaeum's Medal of Honor. Collection consists of personal and biographical information, information on Coro de UPR, Instituto de Cultura Puertorriqueños and music programs. There are also newspaper articles, audiotapes, 43 phonographic records, artifacts and 132 photographs, which include photos of Willie Rodríguez.

Topics: Music; Culture; Leaders and Organizations

| 📅 1910-1987 | 📦 0.5 | 💿 5 | 🔍 Inventory |

The Camille Rodriguez Collection

Camille Rodriguez was Centro Administrator and researcher of the Higher Education Task Force. The collection includes posters, programs and other materials.

Topics: Visual Arts

| 📅 1975-2000 | 📦 8.0 | 💿 1 | 🔍 Aavilable |

A pediatrician, public health leader and women's rights activist, The Helen Rodríguez-Trías Papers offer information and insight on the personal and professional life of a dynamic, charismatic and multifaceted Puerto Rican pediatrician, activist and community health advocate. The collection is a source for study on the development of a Latina perspective in the broad areas of public health, women's rights and reproductive health.

Among the highlights of the collection are numerous biographical articles and profiles on Rodríguez-Trías, obituaries and tributes in print and video formats published or released after her death in 2001, many of her writings and public presentations of the 1980s and 1990s, materials related to her candidacy and presidency of the American Public Health Association in the early 1990s and a photographic grouping that depicts different stages in her life from the 1960s through 2001.

The collection spans from 1929 to 2002 with the bulk of the papers dating between 1981 and 2001. Its collection is made up of correspondence, clippings, letters, memoranda, programs, awards, flyers, writings, speeches, notes, publications, photographs, videotapes, audiocassettes and slides.

Topics: Health and Community Welfare; Gender and Sexuality; Organizations and Leaders; Social Reform

| 1929-2004 | 3.5 | 144 | Finding Aids |

The Rafael Rodríguez Collection

Collection contains information on the Tito Puente Scholarship Fund, photographs, a photo album, New York-based Latino magazines and concert programs.

Topics: Arts and Culture; Gender and Sexuality

| N/A | 4.0 | 6 | Inventory |

The Robert Rodriguez Collection

Collection contains information on the Tito Puente Scholarship Fund, photographs, a photo album, New York based Latino magazines and concert programs.

Topics: Music; Culture

| 1950s-1980s | 0.5 | 5 | Inventory |

The Sandra Rodríguez Collection

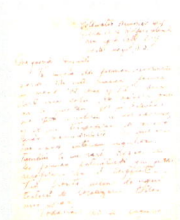

Actress, singer and one of the original members of Pregones Theater. Collection measures 2 cubic feet and contains flyers, programs, postcards, videos, CD's, audiocassettes and numerous books and publications that document not only Rodríguez's career, but also the Puerto Rican/Latino theater scene in New York City. A highlight of the materials is an original letter from Julia de Burgos. Materials date from 1953 to 2005, with the bulk concentrating on the period from the 1980s to 2005.

Topics: Arts; Artist; Music; Culture

| 1953-2005 | 1.0 | 5 | Description |

75

Guitarist and musician whose music expressed the political struggle of Puerto Ricans and the Latino Community in general. Collection measures 1 cubic foot and consists primarily of photographs that document Roldán's performance career. Included as well are a number of photographic negatives. The materials date from the mid-1970s through the late 1990s.

Topics: Culture, Music

1970s-1990s   0.65   1   Inventory

The Mario César Romero Papers

Romero is an art historian, consultant and collector. He was a founder of and participant in various cultural and political organizations. His papers reflect his involvement in these areas and contain rare pamphlets, posters, flyers, correspondence with artists, and an impressive collection of photographs.

Topics: Organizations and Leaders; Family and Community Life; Visual Arts and Culture

1970s-2000s   19.0   6   Inventory

The Rovira Family Collection

The Rovira Family Papers are a genealogy collection consisting of .05 cubic feet of personal documents, including certificates of birth, baptism, marriage, identification, social security benefits and death, as well as various certificates from a masonic fraternity and a document on the masonic moral code, dating from 1935 to 1952. The collection was donated by Angélica Rovira.

Topics: Migration and Settlement; Family and Community Life

1935-1952   0.12   6   Inventory

S-T

Ana Gloria San Antonio
El Mundo
Puertorriqueña de Grandes Méritos

The collection consists of newspaper articles and clippings, newsletters, memos, press releases of Círculo de Escritores y Poetas Iberoamericanos de Nueva York (CEPI, Comité del Desfile de la Hispanidad, and Asociación Puertorriqueña de Escritores (APE). There are copies of El Nacionalista de Puerto Rico and Boletín Oficial and writings concerning the East River North Renewal. Also included are four videocassettes about Desfile de la Hispanidad and poet Susana Cabañas.

Topics: Literature; Organizations and Leaders

| 📅 1944-1994 | 📦 0.5 | 💿 7 | 🔍 Inventory |

The Virginia Sánchez-Korrol Puerto Rican Studies Association Collection

Sánchez-Korrol, professor emerita at Brooklyn College, was a founder member and president of the Puerto Rican Studies Association. This organization brings together scholars, educators, public policy, community activists and students in the field of Puero Ricans in the US. The collection Includes correspondence, flyers, and conference materials.

Topics: Puerto Rican Studies

| 📅 1990s | 📦 1.0 | 💿 1 | 🔍 Inventory |

The Manuel T. Sánchez Papers

ESTA ES SU INVITACION A LA
Iglesia Pentecostal Antioquia
201 Atlantic Ave., Brooklyn, N. Y.

ORDEN DE SERVICIOS
Domingo { Oración y Ayuno 8 A. M.
{ Escuela Dominical 11 A. M.
{ Evangelístico 7:30 P.M.
Martes - Estudio Bíblico 7:30 P.M.
Jueves - Sociedad de Damas 7:30 P.M.
Viernes - Soc. de Caballeros 7:30 P.M.
Sábado - Embajadores de Cristo 7:30 P.M.

Una cordial bienvenida les aguarda a todos.
← Manuel T. Sánchez, Pastor

Reverend Sánchez was the founding member of his church in 1933 and became the pastor of the Antioquía Church from 1934 to 1989 with more than 200 followers. Sánchez officially became a licensed advocate in 1935 and a licensed preacher of the Pentecostal Church in 1939. Sánchez was one of the founders and president of the Spanish Eastern District of the Assemblies of God for 13 years, and was ordained a minister by Reverend Demetrio Bazán, superintendent of the Latin American District Assemblies of God in 1943. The collection is made up primarily of photographs documenting the life and career of Sánchez. Included are transcripts of an oral history interview.

Topics: Religion; Family and Community Life

| 📅 1933-1991 | 📦 1.0 | 💿 477 | 🔍 Inventory |

The Sanromá Pasarell Sound Recording Collection

Puerto Rican born Jesús María Sanromá (1902-1984) was one of America's leading pianists who embarked on an enviable concert career. He was an accompanist, a recording artist, and a teacher, and he also stimulated and commissioned composers to write new music. The audio collection contains public and commercial recordings and interviews.

Topics: Arts; Music; Culture

| 📅 1990s | 📦 3.5 | 💿 1 | 🔍 Inventory |

"El Nuevo Teatro Pobre de América" is a popular theater troupe that performs on the street in marginalized communities in Puerto Rico and in Ny City. Its repertory included domestic violence themes. Santaliz's *El Castillo Interior de Medea Camuñas* was staged in the Jospeh Papp Latin American Festival in NY City, 1992. Santaliz's interest was to express a radical position with respect to the subordinate and persecuted   condition of women in society.

Topics: Arts; Culture

📅 1960s-1990s	📦 0.50	🔴 5	🔍 Inventory

The Santiago Febus Family Collection

The papers are a genealogy collection consisting of 16 family photographs (including *Marine Tiger* and Brazil), newspaper articles and clippings on Puerto Rican Bishop González. There is also an interview of Elsa de Jesus discussing her experiences on the *Marine Tiger*.

Topics: Family and Community Life; Migration and Settlement

📅 1929-1999	📦 0.05	🔴 6	🔍 Inventory

The Santiago Iglesias Educational Society Inc., Collection

The society was formed by members of labor unions from various industries, among them the NY City Central Labor Council, the AFL-CIO, and the International Brother-hood of Electrical Workers, Local Union # 3 to address the needs and concerns of the Puerto Rican and other Hispanic workers and communities in the US. The collection consists of documents, including correspondence, a constitution and by-laws, officer lists, programs and flyers on activities and events, conference/seminar materials, financial records, meeting agendas and minutes, newspaper articles, letterheads and symbols, President José López's file, photographs, and a songbook. This collection complements other collections on the Santiago Iglesias Educational Society.

Topics: Labor and Occupation; Leaders and Organizations

📅 1958-1960s	📦 0.5	🔴 10	🔍 Inventory

The Isaura Santiago Collection

Educator and former President of Hostos Community College. Collection contains information on Vieques, Hispanic voting, reports, a historical calendar of Puerto Rico and an illustrated historical album of the island.

Topics: Education

📅 1976-1994	📦 0.3	🔴 5	🔍 Inventory

Nellie Santiago (Lib/Wor) is the first Puerto Rican from Brooklyn to be elected to the NY State Senate. She represented the 17th Senatorial District of Brooklyn that included the communities of Bedford-Stuyvesant, Brownsville, Bushwich, Cypress Hills, East New York, Greenpoint and Williamsburg. The copies of the bills instroduced and co-sponsored by Santiago span from 1992 to 2002.

Topics: Politics, Organizations and Leaders

| 📅 1992-2002 | 📦 0.4 | 🧭 1 | 🔍 Inventory |

The Petra Santiago Papers

This collection is an important resource for research in grassroots organizing, community activism, and the history of Puerto Ricans on the Lower East Side. The materials document organizations in which Santiago was active, among them the Community Corporation of the Lower East Side, United Organization of Suffolk Street, Council of Puerto Rican Organizations and the Independent Juvenile Baseball League, Inc. There is also information about the Community Area Policy Board. The photographic series is extremely valuable for the visual history it provides of Puerto Ricans in Lower Manhattan. Types of documents include letters, memoranda, publications and programs.

Topics: Family and Community Life; Leaders and Organizations; Health and Community Welfare; social Reform

| 📅 1945-1980s | 📦 4.06 | 🧭 16 | 🔍 Finding Aid |

The Santos Pi Short Stories Collection

Writer. Santos Pi collection includes several short stories

Topics: Arts and Culture, Literature

| 📅 0.1 | 📦 0.05 | 🧭 1 | 🔍 Inventory |

Según Lo Veo Scripts Collection

Según lo Veo was a Spanish public service radio program (WHOM and WADO radio stations) by the migration division of the Puerto Rican Dept. of Labor. The collection consists of resource materials, drafts and final scripts from interviews with Joseph Monserrat, a government official and community leader, who served as director for the migration division from 1951 to 1969, as member and president of the Board of Education of the City of NY from 1969 to 1970, and returned to the migration division in 1989 to help transform it into the Dept. of Community Affairs in the US. In the interviews, Monserrat discusses and advises on issues affecting the Puerto Rican community.

Topics: Communication; Community Life; Health and Community Welfare

| 📅 1955-1962 | 📦 0.12 | 🧭 5 | 🔍 Inventory |

The San Germán Hometown Club was a social community organization located in the Bronx. The collection consists of correspondence, an invitation, an article, photographs of the society's events and activities, including its participation in the Puerto Rican Day Parade.

Topics: Community Life; Community Welfare

📅 1960's   📦 0.20   🗂 5   🔍 Inventory

The Clemente Soto Vélez and Amanda Soto Vélez Papers

Groundbreaking poet, founding member of the literary movement Atalayismo and one of the most significant and revered contemporary Puerto Rican writers. The collection depicts the life and work of Soto Vélez, the cultural life and intellectual pursuits of Puerto Ricans and other Latinos in NY City and for the information it contains on literary circles and contemporary writers who were influenced by Soto Vélez such as Víctor Fernández Fragoso and Martín Espada. The documents are a valuable source for research on the avant-garde Atalayismo movement and the literary history of Puerto Rico, as well as on Hispanic American literature in the US, and various New York organizations. There is also information on the Nationalist Party of Puerto Rico and pro-independence politics. There are also documents pertaining to his wife, Amanda Vélez and his son, Clemente Soto, Jr. The types of documents included are personal letters, poetry, manuscripts, biographies, interviews, speeches and materials about cultural and political organizations.

Topics: Arts; Literature; Culture; Organizations and Leaders; Social Reform; Politics, Government, and Law

📅 1924-1996   📦 9.55   🗂 128   🔍 Finding Aid

The Jorge Soto Collection

Soto was a Puerto Rican painter born in El Barrio. As a member and coordinator of Taller Boricua, a graphic artist collective organization, he was responsible for developing and fostering a new generation of Latino painters. The collection consists of documents titled El Paquete, an artistic collection of various drawings, and sketches and writings on both personal and political topics that formed part of an exhibit on the painter. Soto's works provide us with information about himself and the collective.

Topics: Arts; Culture

📅 1984-1989   📦 0.12   🗂 6   🔍 Inventory

Spanish-American War Glass Slides Collection

The Spanish-Cuban American War Glass Slides Collection consists of 20 glass slides of scenes from this war, which resulted in Puerto Rico becoming U.S. territory. Included are military figures such as Admiral George Dewey, who commanded the military forces for the U.S., and General Joseph Wheeler, the wreck of the Battleship Maine in Havana, and the Battle of San Juan Hill, as well as President McKinley's visit to hospitals and medical figures such as nurse Clara Barton, first President of the American Red Cross and U.S. Army physician Major Walter Reed, whose experiments led to the discovery of the cause of Yellow Fever.

Topics: History; Leaders and Organizations

📅 1900s   📦 0.05   🗂 1   🔍 Inventory

Stereocards became popular in the mid-1880s. They were two almost identical pictures, mounted on a stiff cardboard backing so that, when viewed through a stereoscope, a three-dimensional picture could be seen. These cards became popular in the mid 1880s and were made in quantity through the 1930s. The Centro Stereocards Collection consists of 22 items, dating from 1898 to the 1920s. The cards are of various scenes in Puerto Rican towns, among them Yauco Adjuntas, Aguadilla and Mayagüez, and depict living conditions and economic activities, such as sugar cane and coffee. Typical of this time period, some of the stereocards have racist overtones. Also included are photographs of Major-General Nelson A. Miles, who led the American troops during the invasion of Puerto Rico in 1898, and Admiral William T. Sampson, who commanded the expedition that bombarded San Juan in the same year.

Topics: Politics, Organizations and Leaders

| 1898-1920s | 0.05 | 1 | Inventory |

Stutz was an activist in the movement for school decentralization and an active member of EQUAL, an organization devoted to improving and integrating the New York City public schools. Collection contains materials on EQUAL, school decentralization and the United Bronx Parents. Other documents of interest include statements from staff members of the education division of the Migration Division on school decentralization and files on the People's Board of Education whose members also included Evelina Antonetty, founder of UBP. Inventory available

Topics: Education; Social Reform

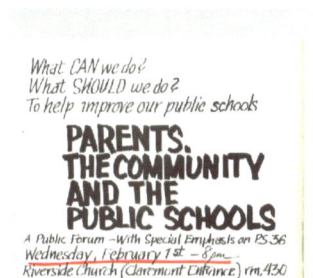

What CAN we do?
What SHOULD we do?
To help improve our public schools

PARENTS,
THE COMMUNITY
AND THE
PUBLIC SCHOOLS
A Public Forum —With Special Emphasis on P.S. 36
Wednesday, February 1st – 8pm
Riverside Church (Claremont Entrance) rm. 430

| 1970s | 2.0 | 8 | Inventory |

Los Sures (Southside United Housing Development Fund Corporation) Collection

LOS SURES
SOUTHSIDE
UNITED HOUSING
DEVELOPMENT
FUND, INC.
1972-1982

Los Sures undertook the daunting task of rebuilding its community, the southside of Williamsburg, Brooklyn. The community residents who started the organization were responding to an epidemic of landlord abandonment, withdrawal of city services and illegal evictions by landlords. Illegal evictions included some property owners who were trying to vacate their buildings in order to change the ethnic composition of the neighborhood. In 1975, Los Sures became the first community-based organization to enter into agreements to manage city-owned properties a few years later. Los Sures is regarded as a pioneer in both the management and development of low-income housing.

Topics: Community Life; Community Welfare, Organizations and Leaders

| 1992-1998 | 0.12 | 1 | Inventory |

Artificial T-Shirts Collection grouped by provenance. Among donors are Diana Caballero and Blase Camacho Souza. These collections of printed T-Shirts promote an array of topics and issues concerning the Puerto Rican communities such as: voting and registration campaigns, Labor groups, Puerto Rican Hawaii Centenenial Anniversary, March for Justice in Washington, Boycott to Fort Apache film, and many others.

Topics: Community Life; Community Welfare

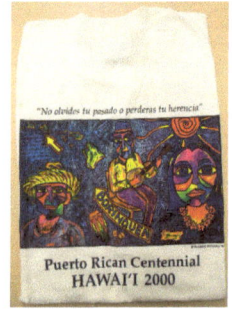

Puerto Rican Centennial
HAWAI'I 2000

| 📅 1984-2005 | 📦 0.20 | ⏱ 4 | 🔍 Inventory |

The Torres-Ortiz Family Papers

The family constisted of businesspeople from Puerto Rico who migrated to New York City and San Francisco. The papers include correspondence, newspaper articles, books, notebooks, magazines, religious keepsakes and other items from each of the family members, the family's steamship voyage between New York and Puerto Rico along with Victor M.'s scrapbook about his military service during the World War II period. Inventory available.

Topics: Family and Community Life

| 📅 1911-1975 | 📦 3.50 | ⏱ 22 | 🔍 Inventory |

The Andrés Torres Collection

Professor, economist and activist. Collections contains materials on the Puerto Rican Studies Association, the Centro de Estudios Puertorriqueños and the National Puerto Rican Association.

Topics: Education; Business; Organizations and Leaders; Politics, Government, and Law

| 📅 1987-2004 | 📦 1.0 | ⏱ 10 | 🔍 Inventory |

The Austin Torres Fiesta de San Juan and Hispanic Day Parade Slide Collection:

Made up of close to 80 slides, this collection of materials documents the Spanish Day Parade (1958) and the Fiesta de San Juan (1959).

Topics: Culture; Family and Community Life

| 📅 1958-1959 | 📦 0.12 | ⏱ 10 | 🔍 Inventory |

Judge of the Family Court in the Bronx and the second Puerto Rican elected to the New York State Assembly and the first to hold the office from the Bronx. Serving from 1953-1962, Torres initially represented the 5th Assembly District of Bronx County and would go on to represent the 4th Assembly District for the rest of his years in office; both districts were located in the South Bronx. From 1963-1967, shortly after the end of his terms in office, he also served as a judge. The Felipe N. Torres Papers help chronicle the long and dynamic career one of New York's original Puerto Rican *pioneros* in the legal and political fields. Moreover, they help trace the origins of the Puerto Rican community in New York in the early decades of the twentieth century and its subsequent growing presence and influence in numerous aspects of political and civic life.

A historically rich collection, highlights of the papers include extensive correspondence with noted figures, as well as memoranda, photographs, flyers, clippings, programs, videotapes, audiocassettes and artifacts.

Topics: Politics; Family and Community Life; Migration and Settlement; Organizations and Leaders; Government, and Law, Social Reform

📅 1881-2004   📦 18.0   ⏱ 22   🔍 Finding Aid

Supreme Court Judge, civic leader and legislator. The Frank Torres Papers document his contributions as well as those of other members of his distinguished New York "pioneer" family in the legal, political, and religious spheres and their overall service to the community. They are especially significant for understanding the groundbreaking role played by Frank Torres and his father, Felipe N. Torres in the judiciary. Among the prominent names appearing in the collection are his father, Felipe N. Torres, Congressmen Herman Badillo and Robert Garcia, and former Archbishop of Puerto Rico Roberto O. González. The collection consists primarily of personal, judicial and administrative documents. Contained are letters, programs, legal briefs, minutes, essays and proposals for community projects, and newspaper clippings. Finding Aids in English and Sapnish available

Topics: Politics; Government, and Law, Family and Community Life; Organizations and Leaders; Social Reform

📅 1917-2000   📦 15.65   ⏱ 24   🔍 Finding Aid

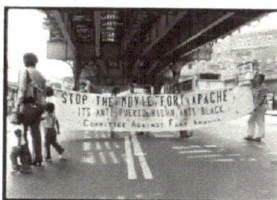

Community activist, educator and organizer. The collection is a source for understanding the role of Puerto Rican activists in the 1980-1990s in New York, the struggles for civil rights of the Puerto Rican community, the National Congress for Puerto Rican Rights, and the Committee Against Fort Apache. There is also information about bilingual education, and other organizations committed to civil rights goals. The types of materials included are reports, flyers, letters and memoranda, press releases and news clippings, as well as photographs.This collection is important for examining the struggles for civil rights of the Puerto Rican community in New York, the history of the National Congress for Puerto Rican Rights and the Committee Against Fort Apache.

Topics: Family and Community Life; Organizations and Leaders; Politics, Government, and Law; Social Reform

📅 1968-2000   📦 7.13   ⏱ 1   🔍 Inventory

Poet and artist. Collection of several art books donated by Tanya Torres. Included are some of her works (*Cuerpo de batalla*) and ohers done in collaboration with poet Yarisa Colon such as: *Imagenes femeninas*.

Topics: Visual Arts; Arts and Culture

📅 2002-2011   📦 0.5   🕐 1   🔍 Inventory

The Susana Torruellas-Leval Art Catalog Collection

Former director of El Museo del Barrio and author. The Collection consists of art catalogs about Puerto Rican artists. Inventory available

Topics: Arts; History; Community Life; Women Leaders

📅 1977-2005   📦 1.0   🕐 7   🔍 Inventory

The Nitza Tufiño Collection

Artist and first female artist of the Taller Boricua since 1970. She is also memeber of El Consejo Gráfico, a national coalition of latino printmaking workshops and individual print makers. The collection includes photographs, correspondence, miscellaneous materials and a video recording of an event/reading at the Nuyorican Poets Café in 1983. Poets include Miguel Piñero, María Mar and Miguel Algarín.The Nuyorican Poets Café has served as a venue for emerging Nuyorican (Puerto Rican) artists and writers in New York.

Topics: Literature; Organizations and Leaders

📅 1950s-2010   📦 0.5   🕐 18   🔍 Inventory

U-Z

The United Bronx Parents, Inc., Records

The records are an important resource for anyone studying the development of Puerto Rican community-based organizations in New York City. They provide information on education and the public school system, community empowerment, local politics, the South Bronx, and the Puerto Rican leadership of NY City in the 1960s and 1970s. Also documented is the career of the organization's founder, Evelina López Antonetty. Types of documents included are correspondence, memoranda, minutes, by-laws, papers, photographs, flyers and clippings.

Topics: Education; Organizations and Leaders

| 📅 1966-1989 | 📦 12.0 | 🕐 50 | 🔍 Finding Aid |

The Usera Family Papers

Made up of a series of photographs, as well as copies of the university diplomas of several Usera family members and a narrative written for Juan Gonzalez.

Topics: Family Life

USERA
FAMILY PAPERS

| 📅 1956-2003 | 📦 0.12 | 🕐 0 | 🔍 Description |

The John M. Valentín Collection

Social worker and former Director of ASPIRA of New York, Bronx and Manhattan centers and the Puerto Rican Arts Guild. Collection comprises certificates, photographs, correspondence, clippings and resumes/biographical information. Included as well are documents on ASPIRA of NY and the Puerto Rican Arts Guild, maps and promotional materials pertaining to Puerto Rico.

Topics: Organizations and Leaders

| 📅 1957-2003 | 📦 0.50 | 🕐 5 | 🔍 Inventory |

The Erasmo Vando Papers

Activist, writer, actor, producer and journalist. These papers are an important resource for studying the evolution of the Puerto Rican community in New York from 1919 to 1945 and also support research on organizational development and cultural and socio-political activities. The papers also shed light on the life and contributions of individuals such as political leader Gilberto Concepción de Gracia, chronicler and activist Bernardo Vega and poet/dramatist Gonzalo O'Neill. They include correspondence, writings, flyers, programs, photographs and news clippings.

Topics: Arts; Culture; Family and Community Life; Health and Community Welfare; Organizations and Leaders; Social Reform; Politics, Government, and Law

| 📅 1917-1996 | 📦 3.0 | 🕐 69 | 🔍 Finding Aid |

Writer and poet, Lourdes Vázquez was born in Puerto Rico.The collection includes correspondence, writings, publications, flyers, press releases, event programs, information and writings by other Puerto Rican writers, clippings, artifacts, photographs and audiocassettes. Included as well are a number of chapbooks and other literary publications.

Topics: Arts, Architecture and Culture

📅 1965-2005   📦 5.5   🕐 7   🔍 Description

The Edgardo Vega Yunqué Papers

This collection documents the life and literary development of Vega Yunqué through several drafts of works, from handwritten notes to published work. It contains drafts of published novels such as *No Matter How Much You Promise to Cook* or *Pay the Rent You Blew it Cauze Bill Bailey Ain't Never Coming Home Again* and *Blood Fugues*, as well as unpublished essays, novels, and poems. There is also considerable information on the birth and development of the Clemente Soto Vélez Cultural and Educational Center, the artistic organization that Vega founded and served as its first director. The collection contains correspondence, photographs, audio and visual files, artifacts and a small oversize collection.

Topics: Family and Community Life

📅 1911-1975   📦 3.50   🕐 22   🔍 Finding Aid

The José Velázquez Papers

The Papers are a rich source of information for researchers examining the Puerto Rican leftist movement that flourished in the late 1960s through the late 1970s and early 1980s. The collection's particular strength is in the documents and images relating to the Partido Socialista Puertorriqueño and its U.S. branch in NY City, the Comité Seccional that Velázquez served in as an active member and leader. Also among the materials are court records stemming from Velázquez's challenge to a charge of violating the Selective Service Act on political grounds, which offer various arguments against the conscription of Puerto Ricans in the US Armed Forces. The collection includes a copy of the file the FBI kept on him once they identified him as member of a revolutionary organization, which lends insight into the FBI's tactics and the degree to which they deemed Velázquez, and the PSP in general, a threat to national security.

The materials include correspondence, clippings, flyers, letters, memoranda, minutes, negatives, newsletters, notes, programs, publications, photographs, speeches and writings.

Topics: Education; Business; Organizations and Leaders; Politics, Government, and Law

📅 1950s-1999   📦 5.5   🕐 4   🔍 Finding Aid

Collection of 12 prints from the Bomba and plena series by artists Lorenzo Homar and Rafael Tufiño.

Topics: Visual Arts; Culture

1950s   0.25   1   Inventory

This collection is valuable for examining the history of the independence movement, especially the history of the Nationalist Party, the Partido Independentista de Puerto Rico and Movimiento Pro Independencia. It is of particular importance for the insight it offers on the role of women in the independence movement and on women activists. The collection also contains significant information about political repression and the persecution of political activists in Puerto Rico. Like many other pro-independence sympathizers de Vando was subjected to years of police surveillance. Among her papers is a voluminous carpeta, the secret file on her compiled by the Police of Puerto Rico. In it are detailed accounts of all her activities, including her speeches at different forums and demonstrations.The collection consists primarily of letters, articles, photographs, police reports, audiotapes, programs and flyers.

Topics: Family and Community Life; Organizations and Leaders; Politics, Government and Law; Social Reform; Women;

1919-1999   5.44   29   Inventory

The Velez-Mitchell Papers belonging to dancer, actress, theatre director, poet and former President of the Puerto Rican Writers Association, contain correspondence, poetry, clippings, press releases, event programs, photographs and videos.

Topics: Arts and Culture; Organizations and Leaders;

1950s-2013   3.40   10   Inventory

Arquitect and art collector, Vidal began volunteering in the Centro Library and Archives in 2003 and was the "Centro Gallery" curator for twenty exhibitions from 2003 to 2006. Throughout these years he donated Puerto Rican artists catalogs, brochures and other documents.

Topics: Visual Arts; Culture

2003-2006   0.5   1   Inventory

A native of New York City, Andino was the grandson of the Puerto Rican composer Julian Andino and was a painter and veteran of World War II. The collection includes pamphlets, writings, notebooks, clippings and flyers that attest to his interest in leftist/Marxist politics, the plight of African Americans in the twentieth century, the social and economic conditions of Puerto Ricans both in the US and on the island, as well as his ongoing concern with issues of race and class. The papers also highlight the intersections between Puerto Rican and African- American communities in New York, and the forging of mutually beneficial alliances across racial and ethnic lines.

Topics: Politics, Culture, Organizations and Leaders

1940-1990s	17	1	Inventory

Visiones NBC Records

Visiones: Latino Arts & Culture is the first PBS series to focus exclusively on Latino artistic expression in the U.S. It examines the nation's diverse Latino communities and how they have been able to keep their artistic expressions alive while creating new and unique visions that contribute to art in America.

Topics: Arts; Culture; Education

1983-1991	2.0	6	Inventory

Vistas Latinas Collection

Founded in 1989 by Miriam Hernández and Regina Araujo, Vistas Latinas sought to counter the disproportionately small representation of Latina artists in museums, collections and galleries by organizing exhibitions and related events, as well as publishing exhibition catalogues and maintaining a slide registry. Collection includes correspondence, artist's slides, mailing lists, grant applications and newspaper clippings, focusing on artistic activity in the New York metropolitan area.

Topics: Arts; Architecture and Culture; Gender and Sexuality

1990-1994	2.0	10	Inventory

The Harriet Wagner Papers

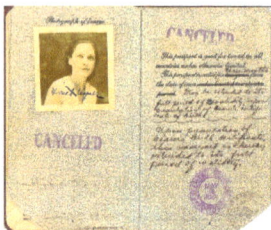

Wagner caused much public controversy on the island when a student who had read from her book manuscript was offended and outraged by Wagner's writings on Puerto Ricans. Collection consists of documents, including official identification, drawings, correspondence (personal and business), clippings, notebooks, travel writings, personal diaries and poetry, as well as 58 photographs and 21 postcards, which include images of Wagner, friends and family, and of Puerto Rico and its citizens.

Topics: Arts and Literature; Family and Community Life

1927	1.0	7	Inventory

Zentella is a central figure in the study of U.S. Latina varieties of Spanish and English, Spanglish, and language socialization in Latino families, a respected critic of the linguistic profiling facilitated by English-only laws and anti-bilingual education legislation. Collection consists of clippings, newspapers, flyers, correspondence and programs about Puerto Rican political prisoners, in particular Lolita Lebrón and the Comité Lolita Lebrón.

Topics: Language; Politics

1974-1979   0.25   12   Inventory

Shared Collections

StoryCorps is one of the largest oral history projects of its kind whose mission is to provide people of all backgrounds and beliefs with the opportunity to record, share, and preserve the stories of our lives. The collection includes audio clips of Puerto Ricans accross the U.S. Collection contains 255 audio files.

Topics: Arts; Culture

2009-2010   0.2   1   Inventory

Welfare Council of Metropolitan Chicago on the Puerto Rican Community

This selection of documents from the Records of the Welfare Council of Metropolitan Chicago in the Chicago History Museum includes clippings, articles, correspondence and minutes; and public statements by some key Puerto Rican government officials like the Governor Muñoz Marín, the Migration Division National Directors Joseph Monserrat and Clarence Senior. The collection also documents the creation of a committee "to promote better integration of Puerto Rican Citizenry into the community."

Topics: Community Welfare; Migration and Settlement; Organizations and Leaders

1951-1976   0.50   1   Inventory

Inventory from Selection of Documents from The American Federation of Labor. Samuel Gompers and William Green

Selection of documents from the Samuel Gompers Papers, former President of the American Federation of Labor, that pertain to Puerto Rico and Puerto Ricans. Original holdings are at the Khell Center for Labor-Management Documentation and Archives at the Cornell University Library

Topics: Labor and Occupation; Leaders and Organizations

1890s-1940s   1.0   1   Inventory

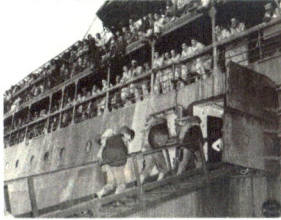

The U.S. Army Center of Military History Contains files pertaining to the 65th Infantry Regiment in the Korean War. It provides "important insights not only into the regiment's unique problems, but also into the status of the United States Army's at one of the most critical junctures in its history."

Topics: Military

1950-1953   6.0   1   Inventory

The FBI Files on Puerto Ricans (Digital files)

An educational project of the Center for Puerto Rican Studies. It contains formerly secret files produced by the Federal Bureau of Investigation (FBI) from the 1930s to the 1990s. The files document FBI surveillance activities and counter-intelligence operations that targeted Puerto Rican organizations and individuals.

Topics: Politics, Government, and Law; Organizations and Leaders

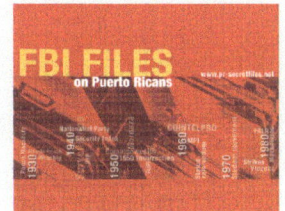

1936-1990s   1.0   1   Inventory

Puerto Ricans in Central Florida 1940's-1980's: A History

This is a Puerto Rican Oral History Project in Central Florida of 95 interviews and digtial photographs. The collection includes interviews, summary transcriptions and digital images and an a traveling exhibition.

Topics: Migration and Settlement, Organizations and Leaders

2008-2009   0.3   1   Inventory

Cultural Foundations of Puerto Rican Orlando/Cimientos Culturales del Orlando Puertorriqueño

An oral history project documenting the stories about two cultural organizations (the Asociación Borinqueña and Casa de Puerto Rico) and growth of the Puerto Rican community in Central Florida . Interviews conducted in English and Spanish and digital images. Collection contains 36 interviews.

Topics: Migration and Settlement, Organizations and Leaders

2012   0.1   1   Inventory

www.ingramcontent.com/pod-product-compliance
Lightning Source LLC
Chambersburg PA
CBHW060814270326

41930CB00002B/39